INSIDER LONDON

A Curated Guide to the Most Stylish Shops, Restaurants, and Cultural Experiences

RACHEL FELDER

HARPER
DESIGN

An Imprint of HarperCollinsPublishers

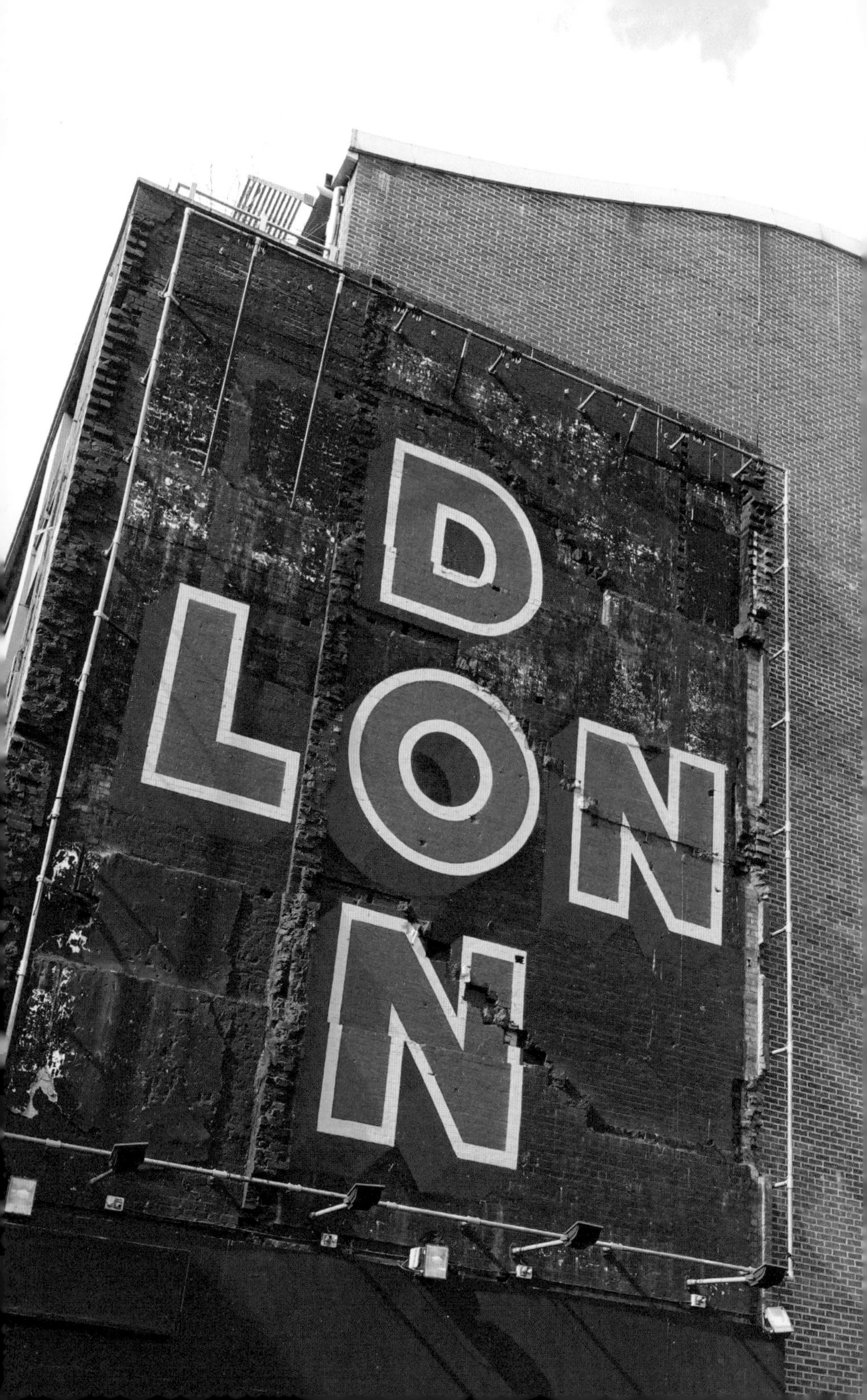
D
LON
N

For Joey Ramone
And his magnificent goddaughter,
Who are both constant inspirations

Contents

INTRODUCTION

WHEN A MAN IS TIRED OF LONDON, HE IS TIRED OF LIFE.

—Samuel Johnson, from *The Life of Samuel Johnson* by James Boswell, 1791

London has long been one of the world's most vibrant, stimulating cities. Lively, multicultural, magnetic, and idiosyncratic, it offers a seemingly endless number of singular pleasures, from the classic to the cutting edge. It's a city in which a deep sense of history and tradition coexists harmoniously with modernity and innovation; it's a global hub of fine art and literature, design and architecture, the performing arts, fashion, and cuisine.

Today, Johnson's canny summation of the city's vitality is more relevant than ever, as is his observation that "if you wish to have a just notion of the magnitude of this city, you must not be satisfied with seeing its great streets and squares, but must survey the innumerable little lanes and courts. It is not in the showy evolutions of buildings, but in the multiplicity of human habitations which are crowded together, that the wonderful immensity of London consists."

Which brings us to *Insider London*. Though London is one of the world's most frequented cities, many visitors don't experience all it has to offer, usually staying within a compact radius of a few miles that includes some well-known landmarks, a handful of museums and theaters, a department store or two, and maybe a chip shop for good measure. A Londoner's London is much more diverse than that, made up of distinctive neighborhoods with individual sensibilities, each characterized by independently owned stores and restaurants as well as residents with a strong sense of community. These days, neighborhoods that were once too rough-and-tumble to attract the masses—such as Shoreditch, Hoxton, Dalston, and

Peckham—are thriving spots for shopping, strolling, and a leisurely brunch. Even in more established, centrally located areas like the West End, wonderful discreet little boutiques and cafés frequently exist, tucked around corners and down tiny streets that many people don't know about.

The goal of this book is to share the best of London's hidden gems and locals' favorites. It's a handpicked compendium of its most charming places, culled from decades of exploring and writing about the city. Some well-known spots are included, but the book is filled mostly with discoveries, all easily reachable by the Underground—also known as the Tube—or the associated Overground network, or simply by walking.

My own love affair with London began many years ago, in my late childhood, when my Stepney Green–born grandmother brought me to England to visit her birthplace for the first time. The city was very different in the late 1970s and early 1980s—the East End didn't have influential gourmet restaurants or an influx of creative cool kids or places to get a soy milk cappuccino. In that era, the British economy was in turmoil—there were workers' strikes, high unemployment rates, and even occasional riots related to deprivation. I was hooked nonetheless: the majestic architecture, the deep history, the accessibility, and even the grit spoke to me. Ever since, keeping a footprint in London, both living here for extended periods and visiting regularly, has been my priority.

Over the years, I have grown to love London more and more, for its uncompromising uniqueness, the ever-present mix of new and old, and all I continue to discover. I hope this book offers an intimate perspective that inspires the same passion in you.

CITY ESSENTIALS

HOTELS

As one of the world's most visited cities, London has a huge number and variety of hotels, many of which have been in business for generations. There are options for every sensibility, whether your taste in accommodation veers toward rooms that bring to mind an Edwardian estate, an urban art deco apartment, or a sleek modernist dwelling. Many travelers are drawn to the city's beloved classic properties—which are also wonderful spots for a cocktail or traditionally served afternoon tea—but there are many impressive newer hotels and boutique-sized charmers too. If you prefer accommodations in a neighborhood where you'll be surrounded mostly by Londoners and very few tourists, there are also inviting and conveniently situated hotels that are a bit more discreet and less well known that will make you feel like a local even if you're visiting the city for the very first time.

Noteworthy Classics

THE BERKELEY

Although the Berkeley is just a few minutes from two major tourist destinations—Hyde Park and the cluster of Knightsbridge stores that includes Harrods and Harvey Nichols—there's something strikingly discreet about it. This five-star hotel possesses a restrained elegance that appeals to loyal international guests, many of whom have been staying in its sleek, art deco–inspired rooms regularly for decades. Londoners who can afford it swear by the spa, which uses products from British brands such as Bamford and OSKIA London, and the gym, which is one of the best in the area. Also of note: the gorgeous rooftop pool under a retractable roof that is opened on warm summer days.

WILTON PLACE . SW1X 7RL 🚇 HYDE PARK CORNER/KNIGHTSBRIDGE ☎ 020 7235 6000
🌐 THE-BERKELEY.CO.UK

BROWN'S HOTEL

Open since 1837 and London's first hotel, Brown's possesses an almost tangible feeling of heritage. Some of that old-world resonance is architectural, as the hotel is made up of eleven Georgian town houses and includes details such as a lobby floored with precisely laid antique tiles and a high arched ceiling in the reception finished with classic molding. It also happens to have a rich legacy of renowned guests, including Oscar Wilde, Rudyard Kipling, Agatha Christie, and Theodore Roosevelt. Although there are well over a hundred rooms, the hotel has a distinctly homey feel; the upholstered headboards and comfortable furniture in the extremely spacious rooms suggest the living quarters of an upscale urban home more than a place for visitors to stay for a few nights. Located in the heart of Mayfair, the hotel has two spots that are popular with both guests and locals:

the opulent Donovan Bar, which specializes in cocktails such as a crisp Negroni over ice, and the aptly named English Tea Room, where seventeen varieties of Britain's favorite drink are served with scones, finger sandwiches, and optional glasses of champagne.

33 ALBEMARLE STREET . W1S 4BP 🚇 GREEN PARK ☎ 020 7493 6020
⊕ ROCCOFORTEHOTELS.COM/HOTELS-AND-RESORTS/BROWNS-LONDON

CLARIDGE'S

For many Londoners as well as those who travel to the city regularly, Claridge's is the city's best hotel. In business since 1856, this profoundly elegant Mayfair establishment earns that title for its extremely accommodating service, rooms that are spacious and sumptuous in every aspect of their decor, lavish (if a bit fussy) food and drinks, and an overall sense of grandeur. For Londoners with means—since prices are high—it's a particularly popular destination to celebrate special occasions over leisurely afternoon tea or dinner. Those in the know also head to the hotel's ultradiscreet spa for facials and body treatments that incorporate Sisley's indulgent beauty products.

BROOK STREET . W1K 4HR 🚇 BOND STREET ☎ 020 7629 8860 ⊕ CLARIDGES.CO.UK

DUKES LONDON

The beauty of DUKES is that although it's centrally located—a stone's throw from Green Park—it's quiet and private, sitting in a diminutive recessed mews just behind Piccadilly, away from the fray. Guests who stay here repeatedly— British and international visitors alike—love the comfort-focused luxury of its accommodations, including indulgently soft linens and enormous bathrooms. While the ninety-room hotel is traditionally English—from the decor of its plush public spaces to its menu, with dishes including kippers and Yorkshire pudding— it never feels overly old-fashioned or fusty. Not to miss is the hotel's legendary bar—a favorite haunt of Ian Fleming, the author who created the character James Bond—and world-renowned for its shaken-not-stirred martini; it's a favorite spot for both guests and well-to-do Londoners.

35 ST. JAMES'S PLACE . SW1A 1NY 🚇 GREEN PARK ☎ 020 7491 4840 ⊕ DUKESHOTEL.COM

THE LANESBOROUGH

This well-located grand hotel is an Anglophile's dream: a lavish Regency building with chintz-detailed furnishings in the rooms, staff and doormen in formal uniforms, and a fastidious commitment to making guests feel comfortable. All of that comes at a price: the Lanesborough is known as the most expensive hotel in Great Britain. Nonetheless, there are comparatively affordable ways to enjoy its pleasures, such as relaxing over a lemon-infused Corner Martini in the snug Library Bar.

HYDE PARK CORNER . SW1X 7TA 🚇 HYDE PARK CORNER ☎ 020 7259 5599 ⊕ LANESBOROUGH.COM

MANDARIN ORIENTAL HYDE PARK

Housed in a 1902 Edwardian-style building that was once the Hyde Park Hotel, the Mandarin Oriental's London outpost offers a balance between classical style and contemporary ease. The rooms and the antique-inspired furnishings may bring an old-school British country estate to mind, but the hotel is very much in the here and now, offering fresh green juice, extra-speedy Wi-Fi, and a terrific spa with Asian-influenced treatments and a swimming pool. The restaurants are a buzzing high point for both locals and guests: Bar Boulud serves what may be London's best hamburger (although a delicate plate of coquilles Saint-Jacques is also a not-to-miss); and Dinner, by the acclaimed British chef Heston Blumenthal, offers an extremely inventive menu of historically inspired dishes that may seem a little forced at first glance but are delicious. One standout: succulent chicken breast served with braised lettuce, as it would have been in the seventeenth century.

66 KNIGHTSBRIDGE . SW1X 7LA 🚇 KNIGHTSBRIDGE ☎ 020 7235 2000 ⊕ MANDARINORIENTAL.COM/LONDON

Newcomers, Boutique Hotels, and Discoveries

ACE HOTEL

The rooms at this London outpost of the extra-hip Ace chain in Shoreditch aren't exactly ritzy—they are a bit reminiscent of a stark dorm room or studio apartment circa 1975—but the hotel is popular with trend-conscious guests from all over the world, thanks to a stellar location in thriving Shoreditch and prices that are extremely fair by the city's standards. The lobby lounge is also a magnet for the neighborhood's creative community, who use the large and comfortable space for meetings and its free Wi-Fi.

100 SHOREDITCH HIGH STREET . E1 6JQ 🚇 LIVERPOOL STREET/OLD STREET; SHOREDITCH HIGH STREET
☎ 020 7613 9800 ⊕ ACEHOTEL.COM/LONDON

THE BEAUMONT

Although it's a fairly new hotel, the Beaumont feels like an authentic art deco landmark that's been in business for decades. Conceived by Corbin & King—the duo behind stylish restaurants such as the Wolseley and the Delaunay—the hotel experience is old school in the best way, making guests feels as though they've stepped back in time, with well-trained staff and tremendous attention to detail, from huge, scrumptious dark chocolate bars left at evening turndown to the music of crooners from the 1930s and 1940s as background music in the elevators. The property's clubby restaurant, the Colony Grill Room, is a regular destination for business breakfasts and leisurely dinners for the city's see-and-be-seen; a fluffy Arnold Bennett omelette, with thick flakes of smoked haddock and freshly grated Parmesan cheese, is a specialty served throughout the day. A special extra for guests only: access to the Cub Room, a plush bar tucked behind a door off the lobby.

8 BALDERTON STREET . W1K 6TF 🚇 MARBLE ARCH/BOND STREET ☎ 020 7499 1001 ⊕ THEBEAUMONT.COM

BLAKES

For guests who prefer hotels with an intimate vibe, this row of painted Victorian town houses a mile from South Kensington is an enduring favorite. Each of the forty-five rooms is unique, designed by interior decorator Anouska Hempel to reflect an evocative destination, era, or mood: the Venetian Suite has a four-poster bed detailed with Murano glass, for example, while the Biedermeier Suite is filled with antique furniture from that period, with nineteenth-century prints on the walls. In back, there's a lovely courtyard with umbrella-covered tables and a glass gazebo, making it an ideal spot for afternoon tea or a glass of champagne even when the weather isn't especially warm or sunny.

33 ROLAND GARDENS . SW7 3PF 🚇 SOUTH KENSINGTON/GLOUCESTER ROAD/EARL'S COURT
☎ 020 7370 6701 ⊕ BLAKESHOTELS.COM

THE BOUNDARY ROOMS

Housed in a vast Victorian building on the corner of boutique-lined Redchurch Street in Shoreditch, the Boundary Room's twelve chic rooms sit above the popular Albion café, a neighborhood favorite for sophisticated British comfort food including hearty house-made fish cakes with salmon and hake and, in the morning, fried duck eggs. Each unique room has a decor inspired by a designer, an architect, or a design movement or style, from Charles and Ray Eames to Le Corbusier, from Bauhaus to Shaker—and all are stylish and comfortable. The Boundary Rooftop, the hotel's covered rooftop bar and restaurant, open year-round, offers a chic European menu that includes British oysters and Provençale vegetable salad, plus clear and panoramic views of East London.

2–4 BOUNDARY STREET . E2 7DD 🚇 LIVERPOOL STREET; SHOREDITCH HIGH STREET ☎ 020 7729 1051
⊕ BOUNDARY.LONDON/

CHILTERN FIREHOUSE

Chiltern Firehouse is part of hotelier André Balazs's flair-filled empire, which also includes hot spots like the Chateau Marmont in Los Angeles and The Mercer in New York City. The anchor of a quaint street that's lined with small upscale boutiques, its twenty-six spacious rooms are luxurious yet unpretentious. With furniture and decor that favors clean lines, dark wood, navy, and steel gray, the rooms have a slightly masculine, monied air, as if you had stepped back in time to a wealthy bachelor's apartment in the 1940s. The lively, celebrity-frequented restaurant at this stylish hotel is extremely popular—so much so that it practically overshadows it: many people often aren't aware that there's a hotel upstairs.

1 CHILTERN STREET . W1U 7PA 🚇 BAKER STREET/BOND STREET ☎ 020 7073 7676
⊕ CHILTERNFIREHOUSE.COM

DORSET SQUARE HOTEL

This elegant, unobtrusive thirty-eight-room nineteenth-century town house, located near Baker Street on a quiet street with park views, has a lot of charm. The polished, individually decorated rooms have an appealing hint of English eccentricity to them—one has deep red walls, another pairs a springy floral headboard with autumnal leaf-patterned curtains—that suggest a friend's home more than a hotel. Although the cozy basement dining room, the Potting Shed, serves three meals daily, breakfast is a high point. Guests, many of whom are Europeans who stay regularly, love indulging in an order of Eggs Royale or flaky croissant stuffed with spinach and goat cheese served by the extra-friendly waitstaff.

39–40 DORSET SQUARE . NW1 6QN 🚇 BAKER STREET/MARYLEBONE ☎ 020 7723 7874 ⊕ FIRMDALEHOTELS.COM/HOTELS/LONDON/DORSET-SQUARE-HOTEL/

THE GRAZING GOAT

This understated property—better known for its ground-floor gastropub than for the eight homey hotel rooms upstairs—is reminiscent of a small hotel in the British countryside with its oak doors, antique lighting fixtures, and wooden beams on the ceiling. Still, there's a refinement about the decor—its streamlined furnishings, its use of quiet grays and whites—that's in sync with its location on a sedate street just a few minutes' walk from Marble Arch. In spite of the many dining options nearby, many guests stay in for the well-prepared dishes downstairs, including an airy wild mushroom soufflé and grilled meat accompanied by irresistibly crunchy chips. The Grazing Goat has a similar but smaller sister property, The Orange Public House & Hotel, located at 37 Pimlico Road in Chelsea.

6 NEW QUEBEC STREET . W1H 7RQ 🚇 MARBLE ARCH ☎ 020 7724 7243 ⊕ THEGRAZINGGOAT.CO.UK

HAZLITT'S

This lovely property is an insider's secret, even though it's in the heart of Soho. Originally the home of the eighteenth-century writer and drama and literary critic William Hazlitt, the thirty rooms evoke grandeur, as they are decorated with flourishes such as ornate gilt-framed mirrors, thick brocade curtains, footed tubs in the enormous bathrooms, and beds detailed with beautifully carved mahogany headboards. Despite the bustle outside the discreet entry door, the sensibility is that of a grand country home, which is part of what the regulars here, many of whom treat the property as their London pied-a-terre, love.

6 FRITH STREET . W1D 3JA 🚇 TOTTENHAM COURT ROAD/OXFORD CIRCUS ☎ 020 7434 1771 ⊕ HAZLITTSHOTEL.COM

THE HOXTON, HOLBORN

One of two Hoxton hotels in London, this large property resonates with travelers looking for a London base that's stylish but well located and neither overly fussy nor too expensive. The rooms are understated and comfortable—with dark wood paneling, soft wooden armchairs, and a small humorous detail or two, such as pillows adorned with a hashtag—and range in size from "shoebox," a favorite with cost-conscious business travelers, to "roomy." On the ground floor, a calendar of art shows and talks draws locals and guests regularly.

199–206 HIGH HOLBORN . WC1V 7BD 🚇 HOLBORN ☎ 020 7661 3000
⊕ THEHOXTON.COM/LONDON/HOLBORN

THE LONDON EDITION

With 173 rooms, this hotel is a fairly large property, but it feels boutique-y, with sexy, wood-paneled accommodations and a sense of swankiness and calm that defies its location, just steps away from the throngs of shoppers on busy Oxford Street. The street-level restaurant, Berners Tavern, is popular for business breakfasts and chic dinners as well as midmorning coffee. On weekends, the lobby—complete with its own bar, plenty of seating, and a pool table—is a popular spot to begin a night on the town.

10 BERNERS STREET . W1T 3NP 🚇 OXFORD CIRCUS/TOTTENHAM COURT ROAD ☎ 020 7781 0000
⊕ EDITIONHOTELS.COM/LONDON

MONDRIAN LONDON AT SEA CONTAINERS

This imposing Southbank building houses a hotel decorated by the acclaimed industrial designer Tom Dixon that's as popular for stylized glossy fashion magazine photo shoots as it is for as overnight stays. The lure here is both the decor—with curvy, architectural chairs that look worthy of a spot in a design museum in the public spaces and rooms, bedrooms with heavily lacquered art deco–inspired bedside tables and streamlined brass modernist lamps, and a colorful palette that includes bubble gum pink leather sofas in the Dandelyan bar and an Yves Klein blue sculpture by Dixon in the lobby—and the spectacular views of London that come from its location on the Thames. Those views are also a high point of many of the sleek rooms, some of which have balconies.

20 UPPER GROUND . SE1 9PD 🚇 WATERLOO ☎ 020 3747 1000
⊕ MORGANSHOTELGROUP.COM/MONDRIAN/MONDRIAN-LONDON

THE PORTOBELLO HOTEL

Located in two adjoined town houses near Portobello Road's famous market (page 182) in residential Notting Hill, this inviting, quite private hotel has been the home away from home for rock stars and fashion types looking for comfortable, under-the-radar accommodations for decades. The twenty-one rooms are decorated individually with antiques such as elaborately carved wooden four-poster beds and footed porcelain tubs; some have an intricately patterned wallpaper that underlies the property's comfortable, intimate feel. In the morning, a lovely, low-key breakfast of fruit and flaky pastries is served on vintage porcelain in an airy sitting room, which, in the evening, becomes a place for guests to meet and mingle over drinks served in crystal glasses and light snacks.

22 STANLEY GARDENS . W11 2NG 🚇 NOTTING HILL GATE ☎ 020 7727 2777 ⊕ PORTOBELLOHOTEL.COM

SHOREDITCH HOUSE

Part private members' club, part hotel, and owned by the exclusive Soho House chain, Shoreditch House is nestled in the heart of the community that is its namesake. The hotel's twenty-six clean, well-designed, yet unfussy rooms are serene, with white shutters and wood-paneled walls giving the rooms a cottage-y, old-school feel. Each room also features Soho House's signature appointments, including plug-in kettles, floral porcelain teacups and saucers, and a tin of freshly baked cookies. Hotel guests also have access to the members' amenities: a large gym, rooftop pool, and a lounge floor that serves tasty British food, including irresistible French fries, or chips.

1 EBOR STREET . E1 6AW 🚇 LIVERPOOL STREET/OLD STREET; SHOREDITCH HIGH STREET
☎ 020 7739 5040 ⊕ SHOREDITCHHOUSE.COM

YORK AND ALBANY

This low-key property—nine snug rooms on top of an affiliated pub and restaurant on the edge of Camden—is part of celebrity chef Gordon Ramsey's empire. The place is certainly upscale—with antiques and four-poster beds in the rooms and creamy-centered truffle *arancini* on the dinner menu—but the feel is casual and relaxed. Although it's not exactly centrally located, its proximity to Regent's Park, Camden, and Primrose Hill makes it a lovely base, particularly for a weekend stay.

127–129 PARKWAY . NW1 7PS 🚇 CAMDEN TOWN/CHALK FARM ☎ 020 7387 5700
⊕ GORDONRAMSAYRESTAURANTS.COM/YORK-AND-ALBANY/

MUSEUMS AND GALLERIES

As one of the world's cultural capitals, London has no shortage of spaces that exhibit art, from majestic, centuries-old museums to cutting-edge galleries. The broad scope of what's shown in the city is truly remarkable, from antiquities to legendary masterworks to pieces by emerging artists, from textiles and industrial design to contemporary photography. Earmarking time to explore London's museums and galleries is an essential part of a trip to the city, and it's relatively easy to map out, as many of the city's best museums and galleries are centrally located.

Landmark Institutions

NATIONAL GALLERY

With its outstanding collection of well over two thousand western European paintings from the thirteenth to the early twentieth centuries, the National Gallery is one of the world's finest art museums. It's a place to see seminal works by masters from late medieval and Renaissance Italy to the French Impressionists, from van Eyck, Michelangelo, and Raphael to Rubens, Degas, and van Gogh. But you'll have to choose carefully, as it would take days to see the collection in full! In addition to the permanent collections, there are regular exhibitions that delve into a collective theme or the creations of a single major artist as well as an intensive calendar of brief and extended gallery talks, tours, workshops, and events for both adults and children.

TRAFALGAR SQUARE . WC2N 5DN 🚇 CHARING CROSS ☎ 020 7747 2885 ⊕ NATIONALGALLERY.ORG.UK

NATIONAL PORTRAIT GALLERY

For more than 150 years, this much-loved institution has showcased depictions of British people of note—pop stars, actors, politicians, and royalty among them—in various forms, including painting, photography, and sculpture. With that focus, it's a very accessible museum, even for those who may be intimidated by looking at art. But there's unquestionable substance to the portraits here, even those illustrating celebrities such as Kate Moss or Mick Jagger, whose images are virtually ubiquitous; walking through the bright galleries is always a moving experience. Along with exhibits curated from its permanent collection, there are periodically substantial retrospectives of artists with a penchant for portrait making, such as Man Ray and Alberto Giacometti, or even depictions by various artists of a single personality, such as Audrey Hepburn.

ST. MARTIN'S PLACE . WC2H 0HE 🚇 LEICESTER SQUARE ☎ 020 7306 0055 ⊕ NPG.ORG.UK

NATURAL HISTORY MUSEUM, LONDON

Situated in a monumental building in South Kensington, this British institution houses some 80 million specimens from the natural world, making it one of the world's most important natural history collections. From a live butterfly house with hundreds of species to a film about a daring underwater photographer, along with an array of exhibits throughout the year, the museum offers a varied calendar of shows, activities, courses, and events for all ages. Though a daytime visit is compelling, the night is an even better time to go, as the museum offers evening tours, some helmed by paleontologists, as well as overnight stays for both adults and children, with cocktails and a three-course dinner for grown-ups and a prebedtime flashlight-lit walk through the galleries for kids. The museum also has an ice rink that is open in the winter that's popular with all ages.

CROMWELL ROAD . SW7 5BD 🚇 SOUTH KENSINGTON ☎ 020 7942 5000 ⊕ NHM.AC.UK

ROYAL ACADEMY OF ARTS

Britain's first art school, founded in 1768 by a group of like-minded artists and architects to further the study of art and design, the Royal Academy's diverse calendar of annual shows features the work of masters such as Peter Paul Rubens and Henri Matisse and contemporary artists such as Ai Weiwei and Luc Tuymans. Located in a beautiful and imposing building in the heart of Mayfair, its permanent collection houses numerous memorable pieces, such as Michelangelo's sculpture *Taddei Tondo* and paintings by master artists such as Gainsborough and van Dyck. As the organization's mission has always been to encourage art appreciation and debate, the Summer Exhibition, in which thousands of artists—both unknown and recognized—compete to have their work displayed, is the high point of its calendar.

BURLINGTON HOUSE, PICCADILLY . W1J 0BD 🚇 GREEN PARK/PICCADILLY CIRCUS ☎ 020 7300 8000 ⊕ ROYALACADEMY.ORG.UK

SCIENCE MUSEUM, LONDON

This sizable institution, open since 1857, has more than three hundred thousand holdings comprised of patented inventions and machines, and related material. The wide scope includes precise drawings by Leonardo da Vinci, the first jet engine, triplanes, models of rockets, and more practical items such as old-fashioned film projectors and primitive antique washing machines. The caliber of the exhibits is excellent, and they are very often designed to capture the interest of and inspire those who may not lean toward scientific interests, such as a show on the work of the inventor of photography, William Henry Fox Talbot, or the Clockmakers' Museum. There's also an Imax theater, which screens first-run films, often with action, adventure, or space travel as themes.

EXHIBITION ROAD . SW7 2DD 🚇 SOUTH KENSINGTON ☎ 087 0870 4868 ⊕ SCIENCEMUSEUM.ORG.UK

SOMERSET HOUSE

The stately building in which Somerset House is located was originally built in 1776 to house municipal offices, on the former site of a Tudor palace occupied by various nobility including Queen Elizabeth I. There's still a grandiose feel to the structure, but the contemporary art and design that are displayed here are accessible and frequently grounded in pop culture. In recent years, for example, Hergé's drawings of his famous character, Tintin, have been shown, as well as clothing from the collection of the late fashion editor Isabella Blow and guitars owned by the influential rock band the Jam. In the summer, the huge central courtyard offers outdoor film screenings and concerts by critically acclaimed rock artists such as Laura Mvula and Benjamin Clementine; during the winter holidays, the same open-air expanse is transformed into a festive ice skating rink that's popular with all ages.

THE STRAND . WC2R 1LA 🚇 HOLBORN ☎ 020 7845 4600 ⊕ SOMERSETHOUSE.ORG.UK

TATE BRITAIN

Since it opened in 1897, the mission of Tate Britain has been to showcase the work of influential British artists. Its scope is broad, including paintings from masters from John Constable and John Everett Millais to to Francis Bacon and David Hockney as well as sculptors such as Henry Moore and Barbara Hepworth. Throughout the year, there are substantial exhibitions of note, many with a contemporary British focus, from conceptual art to retrospectives of individual artists. Nonetheless, the museum has a sister institution in London with a dedicated contemporary focus, the Tate Modern, which can be reached via a shuttle boat on the Thames as well as more conventional modes of transportation such as tube or taxi. There are also Tate outposts in Liverpool and the Cornwall town of St. Ives.

MILLBANK . SW1P 4RG 🚇 PIMLICO/VAUXHALL/VICTORIA/WESTMINSTER ☎ 020 7887 8888
⊕ TATE.ORG.UK/VISIT/TATE-BRITAIN

TATE MODERN

The Tate Modern, which opened in 2000, has become one of the world's most important contemporary art museums, exhibiting work created from 1900 through today in a gigantic, light-infused space, once a power station, before being transformed by the renowned architects Herzog & De Meuron. The vast size affords ample room for wings dedicated to specific periods of contemporary art, from surrealism to postwar abstract expressionism. Rotating exhibitions showcase a wide range of artists from Gerhard Richter and Alexander Calder to Mark Rothko and Frank Auerbach. One of its most impressive areas is the Turbine Hall, a monumental open space with eighty-five-foot-high ceilings that is used to house temporary sculpture installations. The Tate's a place where one could easily spend an entire day, but with that much to take in, breaks for a tasty snack or meal in the museum's restaurant and a visit to the large, well-stocked gift shop are a must.

BANKSIDE . SE1 9TG 🚇 BLACKFRIARS/SOUTHWARK ☎ 020 7887 8888
⊕ TATE.ORG.UK/VISIT/TATE-MODERN

V&A MUSEUM OF CHILDHOOD

This large building, located in what's gradually become a trendy and desirable neighborhood, houses the Victoria and Albert Museum's vast collection of kid-related artifacts, from toys and puppets to photographs of children during wartime. It's a perfect place for families to visit, although the museum's remarkably substantial exhibitions, including shows focusing on the lives of immigrant children in Britain and the photographer Julia Margaret Cameron's images of kids, are thought-provoking for audiences of all ages.

CAMBRIDGE HEATH ROAD . E2 9PA 🚇 BETHNAL GREEN ☎ 020 8983 5200 ⊕ VAM.AC.UK/MOC

VICTORIA AND ALBERT MUSEUM

As the world's largest cultural institution dedicated to decorative arts and design, the Victoria and Albert Museum has built a monumental collection of more than four and half million items since it was unveiled by one of its namesakes, Queen Victoria, in 1857. Included are several major areas of collection—clothing, costumes, jewelry, pottery, furniture, and art nouveau objects—along with more than two thousand paintings by masters such as Reynolds, Constable, and Turner. The museum also hosts exhibitions with strong pop culture appeal, such as retrospectives dedicated to David Bowie and influential designers including Alexander McQueen and Vivienne Westwood. At a half-million square feet, the museum merits a daylong visit if you've got the attention span: there's an excellent café for refueling and a large, diversely stocked gift shop.

CROMWELL ROAD . SW7 2RL 🚇 SOUTH KENSINGTON/KNIGHTSBRIDGE ☎ 020 7942 2000 ⊕ VAM.AC.UK

THE WALLACE COLLECTION

Once the home of the Seymour family, who served in Parliament and were also members of the courts of several fifteenth- and sixteenth-century kings, this stately building was donated to the British government to become a museum in 1897 and now exhibits several centuries' worth of the family's impressive art and collectibles. There are more than five thousand items in the collection: paintings by Rembrandt, van Dyck, and Rubens; sixteenth-century bronze busts and eighteenth-century Italian marble sculptures; wood marquetry furniture, including many pieces by André-Charles Boulle; and even full suits of metal armor. The array has the breadth of what one would find in a major museum, but the building's manageable size never gets overwhelming; the slightly out-of-the-way location—despite being an easy stroll from Selfridges—means it's never too crowded. The gracious, sun-infused restaurant is worth making time for, either for a meal or for a perfectly pulled espresso and a slice of almond and apple tarte topped with vanilla ice cream. The name, incidentally, comes from one of the family members, Sir Richard Wallace, who amassed many of the collectibles inside.

HERTFORD HOUSE, MANCHESTER SQUARE . W1U 3BN 🚇 BOND STREET ☎ 020 7563 9500
⊕ WALLACECOLLECTION.ORG

Small and Specialized Museums

CARLYLE'S HOUSE

This museum, an unassuming brick house that was the home of the Scottish philosopher Thomas Carlyle from 1834 until his death in 1881, has been open to the public since 1895. The original furnishings are intact, including a worn leather armchair and pots and pans in the kitchen, so walking through the house provides an authentic glimpse into what London life was like in his day.

24 CHEYNE ROW . SW3 5HL 🚇 SLOANE SQUARE/SOUTH KENSINGTON ☎ 020 7352 7087
🌐 NATIONALTRUST.ORG.UK/CARLYLES-HOUSE

CHARLES DICKENS MUSEUM

While living in this modest Georgian house in Bloomsbury from March 1837 to December 1839, Charles Dickens worked on his novels *Oliver Twist* and *Nicholas Nickleby*. The home is still filled with the author's belongings: hundreds of leather-bound books in glass-fronted shelving, the dining table and chairs at which he sat with his family, Delft blue plates in the kitchen, and—arguably of most importance—the dark wooden desk at which he wrote. The museum also offers a weekly "Dickensian Walk" on Wednesday mornings, during which an expert on the author guides attendees through the streets in which key scenes from Dickens's novels are based.

48 DOUGHTY STREET . WC1N 2LX 🚇 RUSSELL SQUARE/CHANCERY LANE/HOLBORN ☎ 020 7405 21270
🌐 DICKENSMUSEUM.COM

DENNIS SEVERS' HOUSE

In 1979, an American artist, Dennis Severs, purchased this modest Georgian town house and decorated its rooms with antique furniture to re-create the home environment of an imaginary Huguenot family from the 1720s through to the early twentieth century. He turned it into an unusual museum in which he also lived. His goal was to create not a time capsule but an experience of a certain time. And that it certainly is; walking through the space, it's easy to imagine you've stepped back in time, surrounded by thick crimson drapes hung over a four-poster bed, a small candlelit table with flowered bone china cups near a working fireplace filled with burning logs, and a wooden kitchen table on which eggs and cheese are laid out every day to give a sensory impression of a day in the family's life. Although Severs died in 1999, the museum remains exactly as he created it. Though open during the day, it's especially atmospheric during what the museum calls "Silent Night": lamplit evening tours on Mondays, Wednesdays, and Fridays that require booking in advance.

18 FOLGATE STREET . E1 6BX 🚇 LIVERPOOL STREET; SHOREDITCH HIGH STREET
☎ 020 7247 4013 🌐 DENNISSEVERSHOUSE.CO.UK

FASHION AND TEXTILE MUSEUM

Founded by the English fashion designer Zandra Rhodes, this small, modern museum presents a wide range of exhibitions of clothing, jewelry, and other accessories from the late 1950s to today; past shows have focused on everything from garments made from Liberty fabrics to workout wear from the British fitness clothing brand Pineapple. Though this isn't the world's biggest or slickest museum, it is clearly curated with love, frequently spotlighting underappreciated designers such as Tommy Nutter and Thea Porter who wouldn't typically be shown at the V & A. If you're a fashion aficionado, this is a great place to visit; if not, it's worth a stop if you are in the area en route to White Cube or Borough Market.

83 BERMONDSEY STREET . SE1 3XF 🚇 LONDON BRIDGE/BOROUGH ☎ 020 7407 8664 ⊕ FTMLONDON.ORG

THE FREUD MUSEUM

After fleeing Austria in 1938, Sigmund Freud lived in this Hampstead home until his death about a year later. Now a small museum, the house, with its period decorations intact, gives an impression of his refined sensibility through the Egyptian figurines of Isis and Imhotep, ancient Greek vases, the heavy marble ashtray still sitting on his desk, and, of course, his legendary analyst's couch, covered with an ornately loomed ornamental rug. On the first Sunday of every month a Freud expert conducts a tour of the property, relating anecdotes about the doctor as well as his possessions. The museum also hosts an ongoing series of lectures and classes on the workings of the mind, psychoanalysis in general, and Freud's life and career.

20 MARESFIELD GARDENS . NW3 5SX 🚇 FINCHLEY ROAD; FINCHLEY ROAD & FROGNAL ☎ 020 7435 2002 ⊕ FREUD.ORG.UK

THE GEFFRYE MUSEUM OF THE HOME

The Geffrye traces the history of the English interior from the 1600s to today, through a series of fully articulated rooms featuring furniture, art, textiles, and accessories. This grand building is an inviting place to spend the afternoon, with a break from the immersion in decorative history to sample a slice of Spanish tortilla and a chai tea latte in the bright indoor café. The huge, beautifully groomed front lawn is a popular local draw: on sunny days, particularly at lunchtime during the week. On weekends, it's filled with people who live and work nearby.

136 KINGSLAND ROAD . E2 8EA 🚇 OLD STREET/LIVERPOOL STREET; HOXTON ☎ 020 7739 9893 ⊕ GEFFRYE-MUSEUM.ORG.UK

HORNIMAN MUSEUM AND GARDENS

Originally opened in 1901 and designed by the architect Charles Harrison Townsend, this southeast London museum showcases the passionate collection of John Frederick Horniman, the heir to his family's tea fortune. For some, the focal point of a visit to this diverse attraction is its large natural history museum, as well as its vast anthropological and musical instrument collections, culled primarily from Horniman's world travels. But a visit to the Horniman estate offers so much more: situated in a sixteen-acre park, it includes the oldest nature trail in London, a large aquarium with coral reefs and rainforest area, and several display gardens, including the interactive Sound Garden, which was inspired by the museum's instrument collection. On Saturday mornings, an extensive farmers' market sells snacks for an on-site picnic as well as produce to take home. The place is very popular with families, so it's a good idea to go early in the day, especially on weekends and during school holidays.

100 LONDON ROAD . SE23 3PQ 🚇 FOREST HILL ☎ 020 8699 1872 ⊕ HORNIMAN.AC.UK

HUNTERIAN MUSEUM

Open since 1799 and still used by medical students for research, this museum, a division of the Royal College of Surgeons, houses thousands of human and animal anatomy samples, pathology specimens, surgical and dental tools, and a vast collection of related paintings, drawings, and sculpture. The artifacts are varied and fascinating: the skeletons of King George III and his wife, Queen Charlotte, a doctor's logbook from an eighteenth-century slave ship, and detailed engravings from the first edition of *Gray's Anatomy*. In addition to the permanent collection, there are regular exhibits, from a show dedicated to the history of vaccines to a display of paintings of accomplished World War I doctors.

35–43 LINCOLN'S INN FIELDS . WC2A 3PE 🚇 HOLBORN ☎ 020 7405 3474 ⊕ HUNTERIANMUSEUM.ORG

IMPERIAL WAR MUSEUM LONDON

This institution, whose holdings relate to battles from World War I through today, routinely includes inventive complementary exhibitions, such as an examination of the impact of rationing on British fashion during World War II. War buffs will appreciate the permanent collection, as it tends toward more serious objects and artifacts. Under its auspices is also the Churchill War Rooms on King Charles Street, a bunker the prime minister used during World War II.

LAMBETH ROAD . SE1 6HZ 🚇 LAMBETH NORTH/WATERLOO/ELEPHANT AND CASTLE ☎ 020 7416 5000
⊕ IWM.ORG.UK/VISITS/IWM-LONDON

INSTITUTE OF CONTEMPORARY ARTS

Since the mid-1940s, the ICA has displayed cutting-edge art from around the world as well as thought-provoking films, concerts, and lectures. Regularly included in the programming are exhibits of accessible work with a pop culture bent—such as photographs by Juergen Teller and Dennis Morris—as well as pieces by lauded contemporary artists such as Richard Hamilton and Bruce Nauman.

THE MALL . SW1Y 5AH 🚇 CHARING CROSS/PICCADILLY CIRCUS ☎ 020 7930 3647 ⊕ ICA.ORG.UK

JEWISH MUSEUM LONDON

Located in an unassuming row of houses in Camden, the four galleries of this manageable museum focus mostly on the British Jewish experience, with a permanent display dedicated to the Holocaust and a *mikveh*, or ceremonial bath, from the 1200s. More modern views of various aspects of Jewish life are also shown here throughout the year, with exhibitions such as *Moses, Mods and Mr. Fish*, spotlighting the work of 1960s menswear by tailors of the faith, such as Cecil Gee, and a show dedicated to Emil Berliner's invention of vinyl record albums and the gramophone.

RAYMOND BURTON HOUSE, 129–131 ALBERT STREET . NW1 7NB ☒ CAMDEN TOWN ☎ 020 7284 7384 ⊕ JEWISHMUSEUM.ORG.UK

LONDON TRANSPORT MUSEUM

Popular with families, this Covent Garden museum traces the history of London's double-decker buses and subway system, with wonderful vintage vehicles to step inside and engaging exhibits of related subjects such as period Underground posters. The gift shop just inside the entrance is also worth noting—it's a great source of London-centric souvenirs, both predictable and unexpected, such as doormats and dog collars made from old upholstery from seating on the Tube's District line.

COVENT GARDEN PIAZZA . WC2E 7BB ☒ COVENT GARDEN/HOLBORN ☎ 020 7379 6344 ⊕ LTMUSEUM.CO.UK

THE OLD OPERATING THEATRE MUSEUM & HERB GARRET

Located near London Bridge and Borough Market, the main attraction of this modest space is one of the oldest known surviving operating theaters in the world—and the oldest one in the United Kingdom—dating to 1822, before the advent of anesthetics and anesthesia. Also on display is an array of antique tools and other artifacts that were used before the advance of medical science and the development of more "modern" methods of surgery. The museum is somewhat small and is popular with students, so plan a visit early in the day, especially during school holidays.

9A ST. THOMAS STREET . SE1 9RY ☒ LONDON BRIDGE ☎ 020 7188 2679 ⊕ THEGARRET.ORG.UK

THE PHOTOGRAPHERS' GALLERY

Founded in 1971, the Photographers' Gallery was the world's first gallery dedicated solely to artwork in that medium; today its holdings are vast, and as an institution it's more influential than ever. There are regular exhibitions of the work of internationally established and emerging photographers from Jacques Henri Lartigue to Tom Wood, over three large exhibition spaces. But the scope goes well beyond still photography: the way in which the medium interfaces with drawing, digital software, social media, and film is under constant examination through shows such as *Double Take: Drawing and Photography*, which juxtaposed photograms by László Moholy-Nagy with textured etchings by Jolana Havelková and photographs of words by Marcel Broodthaers, as well as in lectures and evening classes. Admission is free, and the airy café is open to non-museumgoers, offering a calm alternative to the many chain coffeehouses nearby.

16–18 RAMILLIES STREET . W1F 7LW 🚇 OXFORD CIRCUS ☎ 020 7087 9300
⊕ THEPHOTOGRAPHERSGALLERY.ORG.UK

POLLOCK'S TOY MUSEUM

A walk through Pollock's feels more like a walk through an elderly relative's long-untouched attic or a rural antiques shop than an urban museum—and that's a big part of its charm. This unpretentious, somewhat fusty old building on a sunny corner in Fitzrovia houses a quirky collection of traditional children's toys from the nineteenth and twentieth centuries, a somewhat ramshackle but still endearing display that stretches across six rooms. Here you'll find puppet theaters, optical and mechanical toys, board games, an array of dolls crafted in everything from wax to porcelain, tea sets, and more. A small, conveniently located place, it makes for a fun, quick visit—and the gift shop is pleasing, too, as it offers reproductions of many vintage toys and games.

1 SCALA STREET . W1T 2HL 🚇 GOODGE STREET ☎ 020 7636 3452 ⊕ POLLOCKSTOYS.COM

THE RAGGED SCHOOL MUSEUM

This former school re-creates a classroom from the 1870s, vividly illustrating the way in which poor children in London were educated in the Victorian era, making it a compelling stop for families and school groups. An actual lesson takes place, led by a suitably strict "teacher" in the dress of the day, on the first Sunday of each month; the space also includes a period kitchen, with utensils laid out for visitors to touch.

46–50 COPPERFIELD ROAD . E3 4RR 🚇 MILE END ☎ 020 8980 6405 ⊕ RAGGEDSCHOOLMUSEUM.ORG.UK

SIR JOHN SOANE'S MUSEUM

Once the home of Sir John Soane, the acclaimed British architect, who designed and built the grand building himself, the building has been a museum since his death in 1837. It houses his vast collection of antiques, paintings by masters such as William Hogarth and J. M. W. Turner, and the ornate furniture that decorated the house when he lived there. For fans of architecture and design, the museum's most alluring treasure is an archive of thirty thousand architectural drawings—both by Soane and by some of his predecessors such as Robert Taylor, who influenced him—as well as models of some of his most noteworthy designs, such as the Bank of England.

13 LINCOLN'S INN FIELDS . WC2A 3BP 🚇 HOLBORN ☎ 020 7405 2107 ⊕ SOANE.ORG

Art Galleries

KATE MACGARRY

This influential gallery, in a nondescript building on a quiet Shoreditch street, showcases boundary-busting contemporary artists such as Olaf Breuning and Jeff Keen. The frequently provocative pieces are in keeping with the neighborhood's forward-thinking sensibility.

27 OLD NICHOL STREET . E2 7HR ♨ LIVERPOOL STREET/OLD STREET; SHOREDITCH HIGH STREET
☎ 020 7613 0515 ⊕ KATEMACGARRY.COM

NEWPORT STREET GALLERY

In an immense building just south of the Thames, British artist Damien Hirst exhibits art from a personal collection that he's been amassing for decades. Much of what is on show is by like-minded contemporary artists with an edge, such as Jeff Koons and Banksy, although Hirst also displays pieces by masters like Francis Bacon. The space includes a buzzing restaurant, Pharmacy 2 (page 210), that's popular with foodies and art lovers, and a gift shop selling art books as well as jewelry and collectibles designed by Hirst as well as contemporaries such as Sue Webster, Tim Noble, and others.

NEWPORT STREET . SE11 6AJ ♨ VAUXHALL/LAMBETH NORTH/PIMLICO/ST. JAMES'S PARK
☎ 020 3141 9320 ⊕ NEWPORTSTREETGALLERY.COM

SAATCHI GALLERY

The focus of this seventy-thousand-square-foot Chelsea gallery is contemporary art; since opening in 1985, it has championed provocative artists such as Cecily Brown, Gavin Turk, Rachel Whiteread, and, in the early days of his career, Damien Hirst. Saatchi also regularly shows the work of highly collectible modern masters, such as Cy Twombly and Sol LeWitt. Though the building is imposing, the airy rooms inside aren't stuffy or intimidating; much of what is shown here—such as *Exhibitionism*, a huge display of the Rolling Stones' belongings and memorabilia, and a show of Andy Warhol's silk screens—is similarly accessible, even for those who don't consider themselves art connoisseurs. Although it's big, the gallery can get crowded, so weekday mornings are the best time to visit.

DUKE OF YORK'S HEADQUARTERS, KING'S ROAD . SW3 4RY ♨ SLOANE SQUARE ☎ 020 7811 3070
⊕ SAATCHIGALLERY.COM

THE SERPENTINE GALLERIES

Located in Kensington Gardens in Hyde Park and a short walk from each other over a bridge crossing the Serpentine Lake, for which they are named, the Serpentine Gallery and its sister, the Serpentine Sackler Gallery, host noteworthy exhibits of work by contemporary artists such as Leon Golub, Duane Hansen, and Marisa Merz. A former tea pavilion built in 1933 houses the main gallery, while the Serpentine Sackler, a former gunpowder store built in 1805, was designed by Zaha Hadid Architects and opened to the public in 2013. The galleries also offer educational and public programs.

KENSINGTON GARDENS . W2 3XA AND WEST CARRIAGE DRIVE . W2 2AR 🚇 LANCASTER GATE/ MARBLE ARCH ☎ 020 7402 6075 ⊕ SERPENTINEGALLERIES.ORG

VICTORIA MIRO GALLERY

In business for more than three decades, Victoria Miro is one of Britain's leading art dealers. She has built a reputation for showing cutting-edge and highly collectible artists such as Yayoi Jusama, Kara Walker, and Doug Aitken; she was also the first to show the controversial artists Chris Ofili and Jake and Dinos Chapman. The gallery has a second location in Mayfair at 14 St. George Street.

16 WHARF ROAD . N1 7RW 🚇 ANGEL/OLD STREET ☎ 020 7336 8109 ⊕ VICTORIA-MIRO.COM

WHITECHAPEL GALLERY

Founded in 1901, this influential, forward-thinking gallery has been displaying the work of contemporary artists for more than a century. A pioneering force in the art world, Whitechapel was the first space in the United Kingdom to exhibit Pablo Picasso's landmark painting *Guernica* and the first British gallery to show the work of Jackson Pollock, David Hockney, and Gilbert & George. Today it continues to exhibit the work of challenging, groundbreaking artists across various mediums. There's also a great gift shop—which sells notebooks designed by Tracey Emin and Gabriel Orozco as well as a strong selection of books, posters, and small gifts—and a peaceful glass-walled upstairs reading room of gallery archives that's open to the public. The bright ground-floor café attracts people from the neighborhood as well as art lovers and serves hearty snacks such as macaroni and cheese with Gorgonzola and pancetta, as well as tea, coffee, and cakes.

77–82 WHITECHAPEL HIGH STREET . E1 7QX 🚇 ALDGATE EAST ☎ 020 7522 7888
⊕ WHITECHAPELGALLERY.ORG

WHITE CUBE BERMONDSEY

Jay Jopling's White Cube gallery, which has two locations in London, with the larger on Bermondsey Street, has been instrumental in establishing the careers of many renowned British artists including Damien Hirst and Sarah Morris. The common denominator of everyone whose art he displays—including Gabriel Orozco, Gilbert & George, Andreas Gursky, and Christian Marclay—is a sense of provocative edge. The second location is at 25–26 Mason's Yard in St. James's.

144–152 BERMONDSEY STREET . SE1 3TQ 🚇 BOROUGH/LONDON BRIDGE ☎ 020 7930 5373
⊕ WHITECUBE.COM

PARKS, PUBLIC GARDENS, AND OPEN SPACES

London's beautiful parks offer residents and visitors alike a serene counterpoint to the bustle and excitement that come with being in a major cosmopolitan city. There are eight Royal Parks, collectively about five thousand acres that were once owned by the monarchy and used for recreation, and five of them—Hyde Park and the adjacent Kensington Gardens, St. James's Park, Green Park, and Regent's Park—are located in central London. Of course, each park has distinct features, be they natural, such as a serene lake or a renowned garden, or monumental, such as the ornate Albert Memorial erected by Queen Victoria, but they are all as pleasant for a quick stroll as well as for a full day spent enjoying the outdoors. As in most major cities, London's parks host concerts, festivals, and other outdoor activities throughout the year.

CHELSEA PHYSIC GARDEN

Opened in 1673 by the Worshipful Society of Apothecaries for its students to study the medicinal qualities of plants, this large, walled urban garden contains more than five thousand plant species. There is still an abundance of verdant bushes and stems that have been used in the treatment of everything from headaches to cancer; the Garden of World Medicine, a designated area inside, includes plants that have been used medically in China, New Zealand, and Africa for centuries. On a more basic level, it's simply a tranquil place to take a walk surrounded by blooming, fragrant greenery, even on a cloudy or cool day. Throughout the year there are garden tours as well as talks and classes on a range of plant-related topics, from how to create an indoor garden to painting or photographing plants—all popular events that are worth booking in advance.

66 ROYAL HOSPITAL ROAD . SW3 4HS ⊠ SLOANE SQUARE/SOUTH KENSINGTON ☎ 020 7352 5646
⊕ CHELSEAPHYSICGARDEN.CO.UK

CLAPHAM COMMON

This 220-acre park is best known for its ponds, two of which—Eagle and Mount—welcome amateur fishermen hoping to catch carp or bream. Situated in the south London community of Clapham, it's an oasis for locals more than tourists; the park's two playgrounds are usually filled with families who live nearby.

WINDMILL DRIVE . SW4 9DE ⊠ CLAPHAM COMMON ☎ 020 7926 9000 ⊕ LAMBETH.GOV.UK/PLACES/
CLAPHAM-COMMON

DALSTON EASTERN CURVE GARDEN

This quirky garden—situated on what was once a wide spread of train tracks—is a focal point in a community that's a lively mix of Turkish and Polish immigrants, longtime residents, and recently arrived hipsters drawn to the area for its affordable housing, relaxed feel, and unpretentious spirit. Locals can sign up to grow produce in one of the garden's designated beds or relax in the garden under a large pavilion; there's also a café that serves, among other treats, freshly made lemonade and slices of delectable cakes from the local bakery Coco & Me.

13 DALSTON LANE . E8 3DF 🚇 DALSTON JUNCTION/DALSTON KINGSLAND ☎ NO TELEPHONE
🌐 INFO@DALSTONGARDEN.ORG; DALSTONGARDEN.ORG

GREEN PARK

Despite being in the center of London, with Buckingham Palace at one end, the forty-acre Green Park is impressively serene. Weather permitting, it's an ideal place for a picnic, perhaps picked up from Fortnum & Mason before heading in; or to lounge on one of the striped lawn chairs that are inexpensive to rent within the park's gates.

GREEN PARK . SW1A 2BJ 🚇 GREEN PARK/HYDE PARK CORNER ☎ 0300 061 2350
🌐 ROYALPARKS.ORG.UK/PARKS/GREEN-PARK

HAMPSTEAD HEATH

Only about five miles from the busy West End, Hampstead Heath is a verdant urban oasis. Its nearly eight hundred acres are conducive to long, head-clearing walks, kite flying, and—even on London's many cold and rainy days—swimming, with three large open-air pools where nearby residents get their daily workout, many before work on weekday mornings, even in the autumn and winter.

HAMPSTEAD HEATH . NW5 1QR; NW3 2SY 🚇 BELSIZE PARK; HAMPSTEAD HEATH ☎ 020 7332 3322
🌐 CITYOFLONDON.GOV.UK/THINGS-TO-DO/GREEN-SPACES/HAMPSTEAD-HEATH

HYDE PARK

Designated as a recreational hunting ground by King Henry VIII in 1536, Hyde Park is one of the largest parks in London. At 350 acres and with more than four thousand trees, it almost never feels crowded despite its central location near Knightsbridge and Marble Arch. It's a favorite and accessible destination for visitors, but Londoners come here, too, to ride horses, admire the fragrant blossoms in the rose garden near Hyde Park Corner, or watch the birds by Serpentine Lake. Worth checking out, although it's not always a tranquil spot, is Speakers' Corner, a section of the park's northeast end that has been designated for debate and speeches, often with a political slant, for centuries; George Orwell and Karl Marx are among those who have expressed their views there. There is also a calendar of large-scale events held in the park year-round, including outdoor summer rock concerts and an annual fair, Winter Wonderland, with a Ferris wheel, a large craft market, and cold-weather activities such as ice skating.

HYDE PARK . W2 2UH 🚇 HYDE PARK CORNER/MARBLE ARCH ☎ 0300 061 2000
🌐 ROYALPARKS.ORG.UK/PARKS/HYDE-PARK

KENSINGTON GARDENS

For some visitors, the main attraction of this 265-acre expanse is the Diana, Princess of Wales Memorial Playground, which has been a popular spot for families since it opened in 2000. But there are many other noteworthy destinations within, too, such as the Serpentine Galleries (page 26), a pair of affiliated and excellent art venues that display the work of acclaimed and sometimes unconventional contemporary artists. Also inside: Kensington Palace, which has housed members of the royal family since the 1600s, the Albert Memorial, and the peaceful Round Pond, a wonderful spot at which to sit and reflect or read.

KENSINGTON GARDENS . W2 2UH 🚇 LANCASTER GATE/QUEENSWAY/BAYSWATER/HIGH STREET KENSINGTON ☎ 0300 061 2000 ⊕ ROYALPARKS.ORG.UK/PARKS/KENSINGTON-GARDENS

THE REGENT'S PARK

Stretching toward north London, the Regent's Park isn't as highly frequented as Hyde Park or Kensington Gardens, but it is one of London's most lovely and peaceful green spaces, always worth a visit. The nearly four hundred acres include three playgrounds, a tennis center, an open-air theater, a zoo, and the gorgeous Queen Mary's Gardens, in which more than twelve thousand fragrant roses are planted. Not to miss is Primrose Hill, which, at more than two hundred feet above sea level, offers magnificent views of the center of the city. The Regent's Park is also a favorite spot among locals for dog walking, picnicking, and sometimes celebrity spotting.

REGENTS PARK . NW1 4NR 🚇 REGENTS PARK/BAKER STREET ☎ 0300 061 2300 ⊕ ROYALPARKS.ORG.UK/PARKS/THE-REGENTS-PARK

ST. JAMES'S PARK

St. James's is arguably London's most tourist-laden park, as it's located near Buckingham Palace, with views of Big Ben and the London Eye. Nonetheless, Londoners love to come here too. Spots of note include the Horse Guard Parade, a large ground that often hosts processions, and the Duck Fountain, home to seventeen bird species.

ST JAMES'S PARK . SW1A 2BJ 🚇 ST. JAMES'S PARK ☎ 0300 061 2350 ⊕ ROYALPARKS.ORG.UK/PARKS/ST-JAMESS-PARK

VAUXHALL CITY FARM

In a handful of decidedly untouristy London neighborhoods, such as Kentish Town and Hackney, urban farms offer a taste of the countryside within city limits. Vauxhall's version of this family-friendly city attraction is one of the most appealing, with pigs, rabbits, and alpacas, as well as horses and ponies for riding. Special events, including gardening and cooking lessons, are held for kids during school holidays.

165 TYERS STREET . SE11 5HS 🚇 VAUXHALL ☎ 020 7582 4204 ⊕ VAUXHALLCITYFARM.ORG

VICTORIA PARK

Victoria Park, also called the People's Park, is a huge community-beloved expanse in East London, with acres of lawn, decorative gardens, two playgrounds, tennis courts, a skating park, and more. In the summer, it's the site of noteworthy music festivals such as Field Day and Lovebox, which bring together a variety of rock artists to perform outdoors; at each year's end, a cold-weather fair called Winterville brings in an ice rink, a Christmas market, and a food hall that's heated and covered to combat London's typically wet and windy November and December days.

GROVE ROAD, BOW . E3 5TB 🚇 MILE END ☎ 020 7364 3214 ⊕ TOWERHAMLETS.GOV.UK/LGNL/
LEISURE_AND_CULTURE/PARKS_AND_OPEN_SPACES/VICTORIA_PARK/VICTORIA_PARK.ASPX

LIVE MUSIC VENUES

From the Beatles to Benjamin Britten, Britain has long been the home of many of the world's most acclaimed songwriters, singers, and musicians, so it follows that there's an array of excellent musical venues in London, from formal, beautifully appointed theaters to down-and-dirty rock clubs at which loud performances are watched standing up, possibly with a warm beer in hand. Many, such as the Royal Albert Hall, are landmarks in themselves; others are simply inviting destinations where you can hear talented artists ranging from up-and-comers to superstars perform in front of an audience of engaged fans.

ALEXANDRA PALACE

This grand Victorian venue—opened as a hub for entertainment and leisure activities in 1873 and known fondly to Londoners as the Ally Pally—puts on rock concerts by mainly alternative acts, with artists such as Frank Turner, Chvrches, and Britpop icons Suede. Beyond its music venues, the bucolic grounds include an ice-skating rink, a skating park, a lake with boats for rent shaped like swans and cars, and, on Sunday mornings, an excellent farmers' market.

ALEXANDRA PALACE WAY . N22 7AY 🚇 WOOD GREEN/FINSBURY PARK ☎ 020 8365 2121
⊕ ALEXANDRAPALACE.COM

ELECTRIC BALLROOM

Located in Camden—home of the late Amy Winehouse, who reveled in her neighborhood's mix of rock and roll, young people, and late nights—this long-established club hosts a diverse roster of bands in the evening, as well as daytime fairs focused on music and film memorabilia throughout the year.

184 CAMDEN HIGH STREET . NW1 8QP 🚇 CAMDEN TOWN ☎ 020 7485 9006
⊕ ELECTRICBALLROOM.CO.UK

EVENTIM APOLLO HAMMERSMITH

Over the years, many of rock music's most influential artists have performed at this art deco landmark, including Eric Clapton, Bob Dylan, Elton John, Queen, and David Bowie on his final night as Ziggy Stardust, an event captured on film by the director D. A. Pennebaker in his 1973 film *Ziggy Stardust and the Spiders from Mars*.

45 QUEEN CAROLINE STREET . W6 9QH 🚇 HAMMERSMITH ☎ 020 8563 3800 ⊕ EVENTIMAPOLLO.COM

LONDON COLISEUM

This majestic West End theater, which seats nearly 2,400 people, is home to the English National Opera, which hosts classic and contemporary works from Richard Wagner's *Tristan und Isolde* to Andrew Lloyd Webber's *Sunset Boulevard*. In addition to performances, the Coliseum hosts guided tours and opera-related lectures.

ST. MARTIN'S LANE . WC2N 4ES 🚇 LEICESTER SQUARE/CHARING CROSS/COVENT GARDEN/EMBANKMENT ☎ 020 7845 9300 ⊕ ENO.ORG

O2 ACADEMY BRIXTON

The O2 Academy Brixton is one of London's largest classic rock venues that's not an arena. It accommodates the up to five thousand sweaty fans who come to hear alternative rock most nights of the week. Although it has an excellent sound system, it unquestionably gets quite loud inside, so bringing earplugs—or planning to stand far from the stage and its blaring speakers—is advised.

211 STOCKWELL ROAD . SW9 9SL 🚇 BRIXTON ☎ 020 7771 3000 ⊕ O2ACADEMYBRIXTON.CO.UK

THE O2 ARENA

Part of an enormous entertainment complex, the O2 Arena is the concert hall of choice for superstars such as U2 and Adele. Also on the premises are a multiplex cinema, British chain restaurants such as Nando's and Zizzi, and a bowling alley; major sporting events, such as boxing matches, are also held on-site.

PENINSULA SQUARE . SE10 0DX 🚇 NORTH GREENWICH ☎ 020 8463 2000 ⊕ THEO2.CO.UK

O2 FORUM KENTISH TOWN

Once called the Town & Country Club and originally built as a movie theater in the 1930s, this large venue holds more than two thousand concertgoers. It offers clear sight lines, a potent sound system, and—for those who want an alternate view and some space from the main crowd—a large balcony.

9–17 HIGHGATE ROAD . NW5 1JY 🚇 KENTISH TOWN ☎ 020 3362 4110 ⊕ O2FORUMKENTISHTOWN.CO.UK

ROUNDHOUSE

Over the years, this memorable circular building in Camden has hosted a virtual Who's Who of some of the greatest rock musicians of all time, including the Rolling Stones, Pink Floyd, Jimi Hendrix, David Bowie, and the Clash. It still puts on concerts by potent and popular rock bands in addition to theater and comedy performances, and even modern circuses.

CHALK FARM ROAD . NW1 8EH 🚇 CHALK FARM/CAMDEN TOWN ☎ 0300 678 9222
🌐 ROUNDHOUSE.ORG.UK

ROYAL ALBERT HALL

Attending a performance at this grand South Kensington venue feels like a formal occasion, even if you're seeing a comedy performance rather than classical music, the venue's specialty. The landmark building, completed in 1871, is impressive, with an Italian-style dome topped by a twenty-thousand-square-foot glazed iron roof encircled by an eight-hundred-foot-long Roman-style frieze. Throughout the year, a wide range of performers takes the stage, although a high point is the BBC Henry Wood Promenade Concerts, known as the BBC Proms, an annual eight-week program of daily orchestral classical music concerts held every summer.

KENSINGTON GORE . SW7 2AP 🚇 HIGH STREET KENSINGTON/KNIGHTSBRIDGE/SOUTH KENSINGTON
☎ 020 7589 8212 🌐 ROYALALBERTHALL.COM

ROYAL OPERA HOUSE

The headquarters of both the Royal Opera and Royal Ballet, the Royal Opera House is a place to see first-class performances of both well-known works—such as Mozart's *Le nozze di Figaro* and Tchaikovsky's *The Nutcracker*—and more obscure pieces, such as a modern ballet by the choreographer Liam Scarlett about Frankenstein, and a version of *Orpheus* that sets the extremely dramatic opera in a French music hall in the 1930s. The grand main theater inside seats more than two thousand, and its stellar acoustics make for memorable performances.

BOW STREET . WC2E 9DD 🚇 COVENT GARDEN ☎ 020 7304 4000 🌐 ROH.ORG.UK

SOUTHBANK CENTRE

Situated on the banks of the Thames, this sprawling conglomerate of performance spaces includes impressive venues such as the Queen Elizabeth Hall and the Royal Festival Hall. The latter hosts the eclectic Meltdown Festival, a series of performances curated by a musician of note—Elvis Costello and David Byrne, for example—each summer. Throughout the year, the Southbank also frequently holds themed outdoor events on its grounds, such as the contemporary open-air sculptures, art installations, and pop-up food stalls that were set up as part of the Festival of Love, a summertime program that also included indoor talks and performances relating to romance.

BELVEDERE ROAD . SE1 8XX 🚇 WATERLOO ☎ 020 7960 4200 🌐 SOUTHBANKCENTRE.CO.UK

TROXY

Although these days it puts on a wide range of live performances—from 1980s alternative bands to Ukrainian pop singers—this large Stepney venue was originally an art deco cinema, and the decor still has the distinctive flourishes from that era. Clear acoustics and an eclectic lineup of artists draw in London's most passionate music fans.

490 COMMERCIAL ROAD . E1 0HX 🚇 LIMEHOUSE ☎ 020 7790 9000 ⊕ TROXY.CO.UK

WIGMORE HALL

Since 1917, this lovely concert hall has hosted nearly four hundred live music performances a year, with a heavy concentration on chamber music. The crystal-clear acoustics, manageable size (the venue seats 550), not to mention the grand marble walls that enhance the auditorium, make this a particularly pleasant place to hear a concert. You'll find mostly Londoners here, since Wigmore Hall, in spite of its central location, is off the tourist track.

36 WIGMORE STREET . W1U 2BP 🚇 BOND STREET ☎ 020 7935 2141 ⊕ WIGMORE-HALL.ORG.UK

THEATERS

London has been one of the world's great cultural centers for centuries; it is where Shakespeare's plays premiered and, much later, where Laurence Olivier and John Gielgud built their reputations as two of the world's greatest stage actors of all time, and where British ballerinas Margot Fonteyn and Alicia Markova danced with the Royal Ballet. Naturally, the city has stellar spaces in which to see live performances, ranging from the intimate and unadorned to the large and ornate. Whatever form of music, theater, or dance pleases you, London offers many a place to see a worthy show.

ALMEIDA THEATRE

Because the Almeida is in Islington rather than the theater-dense West End, one might be tempted to overlook it, but don't. It is known for presenting engrossing and often unconventional interpretations of Greek tragedies as well as plays by a wide range of nineteenth- and twentieth-century playwrights.

ALMEIDA STREET . N1 1TA 🚇 ANGEL/HIGHBURY & ISLINGTON; HIGHBURY & ISLINGTON/ESSEX ROAD ☎ 020 7359 4404 ⊕ ALMEIDA.CO.UK

BARBICAN CENTRE

The Barbican is essentially a cultural village, with a trio of performance halls (Barbican Hall, Barbican Theatre, and the much more intimate Pit), a three-screen cinema, an art gallery, an arts-focused library, and spaces for conventions and conferences. The broad scope of performances includes everything from concerts by the London Symphony Orchestra to lighthearted plays for kids.

SILK STREET . EC2Y 8DS 🚇 BARBICAN/MOORGATE/ST. PAUL'S ☎ 020 7638 4141 ⊕ BARBICAN.ORG.UK

DONMAR WAREHOUSE

The productions at this intimate Covent Garden theater include classic plays by master playwrights such as William Shakespeare, Henrik Ibsen, and August Strindberg as well as the work of modern talents such as James Graham. Casts here frequently include A-list film stars. Donmar also offers workshops for drama students and fans.

41 EARLHAM STREET . WC2H 9LX 🚇 COVENT GARDEN ☎ 0844 871 7624 ⊕ DONMARWAREHOUSE.COM

MENIER CHOCOLATE FACTORY

A former chocolate factory, this landmark building now houses a 180-seat theater where musicals are a particular strong point, although plays and stand-up comedy are also on the calendar of events. Also inside is a comfortable restaurant at which—appropriately enough, given the building's history—the specialties are desserts, including an ice cream–topped brownie slathered in chocolate sauce.

53 SOUTHWARK STREET . SE1 1RU 🚇 LONDON BRIDGE ☎ 020 7378 1713
⊕ MENIERCHOCOLATEFACTORY.COM

THE OLD VIC

There's a stateliness to the Old Vic that makes seeing a play here a special event, even for Londoners who come back to see its productions again and again. The roster of productions leans toward highly esteemed playwrights such as Tennessee Williams and Harold Pinter, but less well known writers' work is intermittently thrown into the mix, too.

THE CUT . SE1 8NB 🚇 WATERLOO/SOUTHWARK ☎ 0844 871 7628 ⊕ OLDVICTHEATRE.COM

RICH MIX

"Mix" is the operative word for this unpretentious venue in Shoreditch, as it speaks to the interests of its community—from trendsters to the Indian and Bangladeshi immigrants who have lived here for decades—with programming that includes performances of the work of young playwrights, live world music, stand-up comedy, films, ethnic dance, and poetry.

35–47 BETHNAL GREEN ROAD . E1 6LA 🚇 LIVERPOOL STREET/BETHNAL GREEN; SHOREDITCH HIGH STREET
☎ 020 7613 7498 ⊕ RICHMIX.ORG.UK

ROYAL COURT THEATRE

Since the mid-1950s, this Sloane Square theater has built a global reputation for presenting plays that are sometimes controversial and challenge audiences. The illustrious list of playwrights whose work has been shown here includes John Osborne (whose masterpiece *Look Back in Anger* debuted here in 1953), Samuel Beckett, Bertolt Brecht, and Jean-Paul Sartre. Still, not everything presented here is ultraserious; it is the theater at which the musical *The Rocky Horror Show* was first performed in 1973; in 1975, it was adapted into the film *The Rocky Horror Picture Show*.

SLOANE SQUARE . SW1W 8AS 🚇 SLOANE SQUARE ☎ 020 7565 5000 ⊕ ROYALCOURTTHEATRE.COM

SADLER'S WELLS THEATRE

This mecca for dance lovers has thrived under different roofs since 1683; the current location houses a 1,500-seat theater; a smaller venue, the Lilian Baylis Studio, for more intimate performances; and rehearsal spaces for dancers. The venue hosts diverse dance companies from around the world, including Spain's Paco Peña Flamenco Dance Company, the Cloud Gate Dance Theatre of Taiwan, and an annual festival of hip-hop dance with dancers from around the world. Classical ballet performed by both British and internationally renowned companies is also included in the annual programming.

ROSEBERY AVENUE . EC1R 4TN 🚇 ANGEL ☎ 020 7863 8000 ⊕ SADLERSWELLS.COM

SHAKESPEARE'S GLOBE

This 1,400-seat reconstruction of the famous Globe Theatre, where most of Shakespeare's plays were originally produced, provides an extraordinary opportunity to see a performance of the great playwright's work. Located not far from where the original Globe once stood, the open-air theater is open year-round; wearing warm clothing is usually advisable, although the seats are protected from rain or snow by a sound roof.

21 NEW GLOBE WALK . SE1 9DT 🚇 BLACKFRIARS/MANSION HOUSE/SOUTHWARK/LONDON BRIDGE
☎ 020 7902 1400 ⊕ SHAKESPEARESGLOBE.COM

SHOPS

Although it's been widely contested, Napoleon Bonaparte is said to have referred to England as "a nation of shopkeepers"—a country ill prepared for war. But even if Napoleon didn't actually utter the quip, it's a description that has stuck because it's true, particularly in London, where entrepreneurs and their sometimes offbeat visions make shopping one of the city's most captivating and pleasurable pastimes. In a sense, London's shopping scene mirrors the city itself: a unique hybrid of old and new, down-to-earth practicality and lavish glitz, resolute Britishness and a mélange of cultural traditions of those who have immigrated from around the world. There are stores that look the same way they have for centuries and, often right nearby, upstarts selling the trendiest creations.

DEPARTMENT STORES

For many avid shoppers, the perfect way to spend an afternoon is at a grand department store, wandering through its many rooms of disparate and enticing options, deriving inspiration from the selection, and finding items to purchase or simply covet. There's also a practicality, and a certain economy, to shops of this vast size and scope: they offer an easy and centralized place in which to find gifts and essentials. London's best-known department stores are world-famous destinations; they live up to their reputations of offering impeccable service and a huge choice of well-made items. The city's less renowned multicategory shops are worthy of a visit too; they frequently attract mainly locals and offer less recognized but still impressive brands. Many department stores also feature excellent restaurants, whether a casual café or a more formal dining experience, for refueling and people watching.

Fortnum & Mason

In business since 1707, this food-centric department store is a reliable source of culinary treats, particularly of the singularly British kind: marmalades and jams, cookies, chocolates, and numerous varieties of tea. Locals know to head upstairs to the notable departments of nonedibles, particularly the beauty area, which carries insider brands by the likes of leading facialist Sarah Chapman and podiatrist Margaret Dabbs. They also know to come early in the day, before the ground floor fills up with tourists.

181 PICCADILLY . W1A 1ER 🚇 GREEN PARK/PICCADILLY CIRCUS ☎ 020 7734 8040
🌐 FORTNUMANDMASON.COM

John Lewis

This reliable, understated department store—a favorite of locals, despite its touristy Oxford Street location—is a refreshingly calm place to buy both gifts and essentials. The flagship of a well-respected national chain, John Lewis is where Brits buy home essentials they can depend on—dishes, vacuum cleaners, blankets, electronics, formal school uniforms—although there is a wide selection of clothing and cosmetics, too. It's an ideal place to find authentically British purchases to bring home, such as ceramic egg cups and merino cardigan sweaters, at prices that are extremely fair for the always high quality. Not to miss: the basement food hall, a large branch of the upscale supermarket chain Waitrose, known for its high caliber and extensive range of both fresh and pantry items.

300 OXFORD STREET . W1C 1DX 🚇 OXFORD CIRCUS/BOND STREET ☎ 020 7629 7711
🌐 JOHNLEWIS.COM/OUR-SHOPS/OXFORD-STREET

Liberty

With its grand Tudor-style facade and boutique-y feel, Liberty is one of the world's most charming department stores, with a more curated approach than many shops of its size. Don't miss its most treasured nooks: the well-edited china selection upstairs; Café Liberty, where you might catch a fashion editor in a casual meeting over cups of tea; and the fabric department, where you can buy large swatches of the store's signature patterned textiles, for which it is known worldwide.

REGENT STREET . W1B 5AH 🚇 OXFORD CIRCUS/PICCADILLY CIRCUS ☎ 020 7734 1234
🌐 LIBERTY.CO.UK

Harvey Nichols

Harvey Nichols is as posh and refined as its Knightsbridge location, with a long row of designer boutiques stretching beyond its Sloane Street entrance. This buzzing store is the place to find coveted status brands such as Céline, Givenchy, Gucci, Christian Louboutin, and Marni, and it carries an excellent selection of beauty brands on the ground floor. Upstairs, several restaurants provide prime people watching, especially Kurobata, an outpost of the Japanese eatery that has several other London locations.

109–125 KNIGHTSBRIDGE . SW1X 7RJ 🚇 KNIGHTSBRIDGE ☎ 020 7235 5000
🌐 HARVEYNICHOLS.COM/STORE/KNIGHTSBRIDGE

Selfridges & Co.

Although it's been in business since 1909, this Oxford Street landmark is a decidedly modern retailer, constantly adding hot new brands to every category it carries. Well known for its array of trendy clothing and accessories for both men and women, Selfridges is also an excellent source for home goods, found in the subterranean tabletop department, newly introduced fragrances and cosmetics, and edible treats, sold in the large ground-floor food hall.

400 OXFORD STREET . W1A 1AB 🚇 MARBLE ARCH/BOND STREET ☎ 020 7318 3989
🌐 SELFRIDGES.COM

Harrods

Founded in 1834, Harrods, and the majestic, gilt-finished building it's housed in, is as much an institution as a retail store, which means that if you shop there, you will probably be surrounded by more tourists than Londoners. The store is an enormous emporium that offers a comprehensive array of items from the world's top designer brands. A sense of grandeur infuses the surroundings, with extra-high ceilings, rococo-detailed staircases, and helpful doormen clad in the shop's distinctive shade of moss green. For refueling, there's a surprisingly calm ground-floor branch of the macaron specialist Ladurée, as well as the store's famous food hall, a legendarily lavish department with hundreds of cheeses from all over Europe and beyond, a selection of the finest caviars, glossy and sweet fruit tarts, a potentially overwhelming choice of chocolates, cookies, packaged coffee and tea, and, during holidays throughout the year, a vast and colorful assortment of traditional foods and treats.

87–135 BROMPTON ROAD . SW1X 7XL 🚇 KNIGHTSBRIDGE ☎ 020 7730 1234
🌐 HARRODS.COM

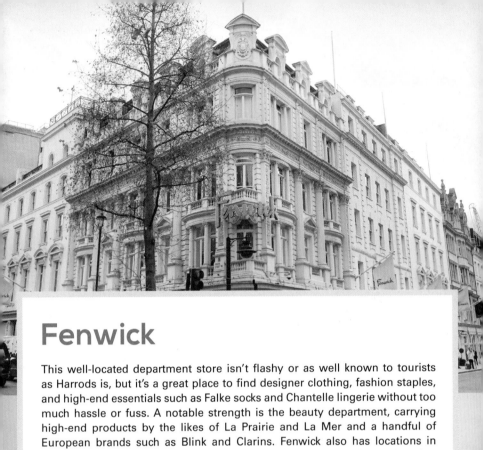

Fenwick

This well-located department store isn't flashy or as well known to tourists as Harrods is, but it's a great place to find designer clothing, fashion staples, and high-end essentials such as Falke socks and Chantelle lingerie without too much hassle or fuss. A notable strength is the beauty department, carrying high-end products by the likes of La Prairie and La Mer and a handful of European brands such as Blink and Clarins. Fenwick also has locations in other, smaller British cities—and an outpost in London's Brent Cross shopping center—but this flagship location is its most comprehensively stocked branch.

63 NEW BOND STREET . W1S 1RQ 🚇 BOND STREET ☎ 020 7629 9161
🌐 FENWICK.CO.UK/STORES/BOND-STREET

CLOTHING AND ACCESSORIES

Walking down the streets of London, it's easy to see, to borrow from the title of a classic Kinks song, "dedicated followers of fashion." London is a city of style lovers, both male and female, from ages eighteen to eighty, from those favoring artist-designed T-shirts and bold jewelry to those who never leave the house without donning a structured wool hat and a handmade pair of leather shoes. As one of the world's fashion capitals, London is a wonderful place to find unique garments and accessories, many sold by the designers themselves in their own boutiques. While many of the city's new and trend-driven stores reflect the pulse of fashion, there are extraordinary heritage fashion shops that are not to be missed for their items of enduring style and craftsmanship; very often these stores sell items that have been made by hand in the same location for decades, even centuries.

LN-CC

Shopping at LN-CC, which stands for "Late Night Chameleon Cafe," feels more like visiting a private club than a designer boutique. Situated on a quiet lane off Dalston's gritty Kingsland High Street, the store is open by appointment only, and scheduled customers are buzzed in through a locked unmarked door. Inside, there's a forward-thinking, expensive mix of pieces and accessories by designer brands, including Rick Owens, Acne Studios, and Saint Laurent, which makes this shop a favorite of stylists and affluent tastemakers. The shop also stocks emerging names such as Eckhaus Latta and Petrucha Studio. You'll also find a selection of art books, some of which are rare and vintage, plus music-related items such as Nagoya turntable needles, Grado Labs headphones, and a concise choice of obscure, mostly electronic, vinyl albums.

18–24 SHACKLEWELL LANE . E8 2EZ 🚇 DALSTON KINGSLAND/DALSTON JUNCTION

☎ 020 7275 7265 🌐 LN-CC.COM

Mouki Mou

The smart edit of brands at this Marylebone boutique is curated by proprietor Maria Lemos, who also owns an influential fashion industry showroom. The selection revolves around discoveries in many categories: fluid dresses by Rachel Comey and Sofie D'Hoore, jewelry from Mikkel Brøgger and Ten Thousand Things, D.S. & Durga's potent perfumes and scented candles, and geek-chic leather shoes by Feit. With a subdued vibe and friendly but never hard-sell staff, Mouki Mou is a very pleasant place to shop. Follow your visit with a coffee or cocktail at Chiltern Firehouse, which is just a few doors down the charming block on which the shop stands.

29 CHILTERN STREET . W1U 7PL 🚇 BAKER STREET ☎ 020 7224 4010
🌐 MOUKIMOU.COM

58.59

Anya Hindmarch Bespoke

Anya Hindmarch's flawlessly crafted leather handbags are renowned among stylish types and sold worldwide; this Chelsea boutique is an insider's secret, offering only custom-made purses, briefcases, and small leather goods, available both plain and embossed with initials, dates, and even little sketches. The decor is more like that of a nineteenth-century men's haberdashery than a modern leather goods boutique, which only serves to make shopping here for one-of-a-kind pieces feel more special. To the right of a large main room with samples and look books is a busy workshop space, where expert apron-clad craftspeople put finishing touches on orders, which can take a few months to complete.

15–17 PONT STREET . SW1X 9EH 🚇 SLOANE SQUARE/KNIGHTSBRIDGE ☎ 020 7838 9177
🌐 ANYAHINDMARCH.COM

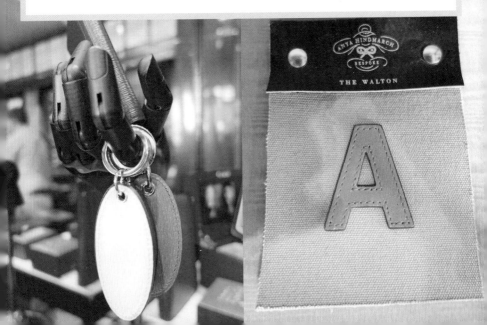

Dover Street Market

For style mavens, Dover Street Market is one of the world's must-see lifestyle stores, like Colette in Paris and 10 Corso Como in Milan. Even for those with high expectations, the salient designer items for both sexes never disappoint. There's an edge to most of the merchandise that's sold here, including pieces by high-end labels such as Thom Browne, Valentino, and Rick Owens; sneakers are also a strength, particularly those that are designer collaborations. The market's owned by Comme des Garçons, so that brand's collections are also on offer, including bright leather wallets and distinctive footwear and clothing. Beyond what's for sale, the sheer spectacle of the store—with dramatic, colorful sculptures peppered throughout—make it worth the trip even if you have no plans to make a purchase. Although the store's name derives from its original address on Mayfair's Dover Street, since 2016 it has been located in a grand Beaux-Arts building near Trafalgar Square that was once Burberry's London flagship store.

18–22 HAYMARKET . SW1Y 4DQ 🚇 CHARING CROSS ☎ 020 7518 0680
🌐 LONDON.DOVERSTREETMARKET.COM

Thethestore

Meryl Fernandes, the founder of this uncluttered store, is a familiar face to many Brits—she is an actress who appeared on the television soap opera *EastEnders* as well as in a handful of London stage productions. Her store is anything but theatrical, though: it's a clean space that offers her globally sourced picks, such as Korean Mizon skincare products, Japanese Studio Cosette jewelry, and Italian Marvis toothpaste. There are British finds here, too, such as canisters of Rare Tea Company's gourmet-approved blends, and scented candles by Earl of East London, which is headquartered nearby. In spite of its trendy location, the store has a relaxed atmosphere that makes it tempting to linger and browse, even though the space is diminutive.

205 HACKNEY ROAD . E2 8JP 🚇 HOXTON ☎ NO TELEPHONE

🌐 THETHESTORE.COM

Pandora Dress Agency

When the savviest women of Knightsbridge are looking for designer bargains, they skip Harrods and Harvey Nichols and head to Cheval Place, a tiny mews a few minutes away, where several excellent consignment stores offer many of the same top-tier brands at a fraction of the price. The cavernous Pandora Dress Agency is the street's biggest and best source of clothing and accessories, including such iconic investments as quilted Chanel bags and Hermès *collier de chien* studded cuffs. Although everything here is delicately used, the condition of the items is usually excellent, with the original—and considerably higher—price tags occasionally still intact.

16–22 CHEVAL PLACE . SW7 1ES 🚇 KNIGHTSBRIDGE/SOUTH KENSINGTON ☎ 020 7589 5289
🌐 PANDORADRESSAGENCY.COM

Ede & Ravenscroft

The name Ede & Ravenscoft might not ring a bell, but chances are that you, along with millions of people worldwide, have seen the work that is sold at this venerable shop. Open since 1689, Ede & Ravenscroft has a long history of making the royal robes for coronations and other ceremonies, serving as tailor and robe maker for Queen Elizabeth II as well as robe maker for the Duke of Edinburgh and the Prince of Wales; the shop also creates legal dress, the customized gowns and wigs that British lawyers wear in court. As expected, the shop has a tangible sense of tradition and reserve, but not everything on offer is prim or formal: there is conservative but wearable clothing, including thick wool suits for men and blazers by Paul Smith and Max Mara for women. There are also menswear branches at 2 Gracechurch Street and 8 Burlington Gardens.

93 CHANCERY LANE . WC2A 1DU 🚇 CHANCERY LANE/HOLBORN ☎ 020 7405 3906
🌐 EDEANDRAVENSCROFT.COM

Couverture & The Garbstore

This enticing multilevel boutique stocks understated designer wear for men and women that resonates with the fashion-conscious Notting Hill crowd. On the main floor, there are easy-to-wear separates by Steven Alan, A Détacher, and Demylee as well as delicate gold jewelry by Brooklyn's Mociun and Madrid's Helena Rohner. Downstairs are house-label guys' printed shirts and sturdy corduroy trousers along with Engineered Garments parkas and spunky tees. The shop also offers kids' clothing with an adult aesthetic; toys, such as bright, handmade stuffed animals and puppets; and a concise pick of home goods. The eager-to-please staff is happy to help with suggestions and try-ons, whether you're shopping for a gift, looking for something specific, or just browsing.

188 KENSINGTON PARK ROAD . W11 2ES 🚇 NOTTING HILL GATE ☎ 020 7229 2178
🌐 COUVERTUREANDTHEGARBSTORE.COM

The Goodhood Store

This sleek Shoreditch retailer is a manageably sized department store of cool. There are clothing and shoes for men and women by designers such as Alexander Wang, Junya Watanabe, and Comme des Garçons; Malin + Goetz shower gel and Escentric Molecules perfume; Iittala drinking glasses and HAY patterned cushions; weighty Tom Wood signet rings and delicate gold earrings by Gabriela Artigas. The prices tend to be on the steep side, although you'll also find classic, more affordable hipster brands, especially in the footwear realm, with labels such as Vans, Converse, and Dr. Martens.

151 CURTAIN ROAD . EC2A 3QE 🚇 OLD STREET ☎ 020 7729 3600
🌐 GOODHOODSTORE.COM

Stephen Jones Millinery

Stephen Jones's hats have been worn by supermodels on fashion show catwalks, royalty at Ascot, pop stars keen to make an impact, and mere mortals at special occasions such as weddings. They've also appeared on many a mannequin in fashion exhibits from the Louvre in Paris to the Metropolitan Museum of Art in New York City. Jones creates true statement pieces, but his work never overwhelms the outfit or the wearer and always suggests a sense of fun alongside the glamour. Since Jones is extremely well known in fashion circles, you might expect that he works in a grand studio and by special order only, but some of his creations are on sale at this jewel-box boutique, which also houses his design workshop in the back.

36 GREAT QUEEN STREET . WC2B 5AA 🚇 COVENT GARDEN/HOLBORN ☎ 020 7242 0770

🌐 STEPHENJONESMILLINERY.COM

Viola

Connaught Street—a small, unpretentious block in a residential area, albeit one that's very near Marble Arch—is the opposite of a tourist thoroughfare. In-the-know locals head there to shop at Viola, a succinct but thoughtfully stocked, cordial boutique that offers a handpicked assortment of highly wearable pieces from respected labels including Raquel Allegra, Bella Freud, L'Agence, and David Szeto. You'll also find delicate gold jewelry by Laura Gravestock and Mary Temperley, and shoes by Philippe Model. Though a few of the items here are in sync with passing trends, it's more of a place to find confident items to wear with pleasure season after season.

25 CONNAUGHT STREET . W2 2AY ⚇ MARBLE ARCH/EDGWARE ROAD ☎ 020 7262 2722
🌐 VIOLALONDON.COM

Hornets

This cluster of four fabulously cluttered stores sells vintage British menswear that harks back to a more formal era of top hats, spats, and suspenders. There are thick woolen striped scarves in colors that designate specific colleges at Cambridge and Oxford Universities, silk cravats, V-necked cricket sweaters, handmade John Lobb shoes, and well-worn vintage Barbour jackets that indisputably look better with age. The quality and condition of everything are extremely high, and the prices are lower than you might expect for such beautifully made pieces, even if they are preworn. The staff is knowledgeable and very helpful, even if you walk in without knowing how to do up a bow tie or the best way to put on cuff links.

2 AND 4 KENSINGTON CHURCH WALK . W8 4NB AND 36B KENSINGTON CHURCH STREET . W8 4BX
🚇 HIGH STREET KENSINGTON ☎ 020 7937 2627 AND 020 7937 1515
🌐 HORNETSKENSINGTON.CO.UK

Cutler and Gross

Decades before logo-laden designer sunglasses became commonplace, Graham Cutler and Tony Gross began offering their distinctive frames in this bright space, where the brand is still sold today. Cutler and Gross is a working optician, where opticals, contact lenses, and sunglasses are all available and eye exams are carried out in a small room in back. Although the frames aren't branded under the store's name as such, they make a statement, as the bold glasses worn by Cutler and Gross fans like I. M. Pei and Elton John demonstrate to great effect. The prices are high, but the glasses are crafted to last. In addition to this flagship location, the brand has a branch at 55 Brushfield Street in Old Spitalfields Market.

16 KNIGHTSBRIDGE GREEN . SW1X 7QL 🚇 KNIGHTSBRIDGE ☎ 020 7581 2250
🌐 CUTLERANDGROSS.COM/LONDON-KNIGHTSBRIDGE

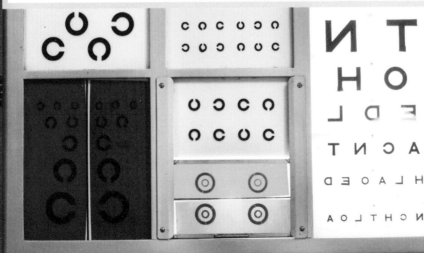

Lock & Co. Hatters

Thanks to film and fiction, a brimmed and structured hat has long been portrayed as a component of a proper British gentleman's attire, yet the image is rooted in reality. Since the late 1600s, upscale Londoners have been buying trilbies, fedoras, and pork pies at Lock & Co., the city's oldest hat maker— and the inventor of the bowler hat in 1849. This stalwart boutique, which sold traditional styles for men only until about twenty-five years ago, now offers items for women: hats, fascinators, and soft ribbed cashmere beanies. The prices are quite high, but the quality and the ultra-accommodating customer service are, too.

6 ST. JAMES'S STREET . SW1A 1EF 🚇 GREEN PARK ☎ 020 7930 8874
🌐 LOCKHATTERS.CO.UK

What Katie Did

The lingerie at this stylized store harks back to the va-va-voom 1940s, an era of back-seamed stockings, garter belts, corsets, and girdles. Even though the shop is in a grounded neighborhood—at the Ladbroke Grove end of Portobello Road, with market stalls right outside on weekends—the selection is decidedly glamorous; the prices, which are more in sync with the surroundings, are extremely fair for the quality. Fit is also a priority, so the well-trained women who work here are happy to spend ample time to help customers make sure everything holds and accentuates in exactly the way it should.

26 PORTOBELLO GREEN, 281 PORTOBELLO ROAD . W10 5TZ 🚇 LADBROKE GROVE
☎ 0345 430 8943 ⊕ WHATKATIEDID.COM

J. W. Beeton

This irresistible West London favorite sells a neat mix of little gifts as well as clothing for men, women, and children; nothing's overly expensive, and everything has a hefty dose of charm. The esthetic revolves around classics with a twist: Breton striped tees embellished with a giant embroidered number, whimsical greeting cards and colorfully bound paper notebooks, patterned Nooki kimonos to wear as robes or summertime outfit toppers, Missoni-inspired totes, and brightly colored cotton socks. Everything is handpicked by owner Debbie Potts, who has operated the store since the late 1990s in a couple different locations.

141 ASKEW ROAD . W12 9AU 🚇 SHEPHERD'S BUSH/STAMFORD BROOK ☎ 020 8743 8118
🌐 JWBEETON.CO.UK

G. J. Cleverley & Co.

This refined boutique, situated inside a nineteenth-century covered arcade in Mayfair, has been selling exquisitely crafted handmade shoes for more than a half century to an elite clientele that includes Hollywood icons and royalty of both sexes. The prices are out of most people's league—custom orders, the specialty here, average several thousand pounds per pair—but those who can afford the bespoke footwear, which is crafted by experts above the shop, swear by the impeccable quality. The store also sells somewhat more affordable ready-made shoes, velvet bedroom slippers, and small leather goods such as belts, wallets, and briefcases.

13 THE ROYAL ARCADE, 28 OLD BOND STREET . W1S 4SL 🚊 GREEN PARK/BOND STREET
☎ 020 7493 0443 ⊕ GJCLEVERLEY.CO.UK

William Vintage

This sleek, appointment-only retail space near Marylebone High Street specializes in the type of vintage clothing typically found in a fashion museum rather than a centrally located boutique: 1960s Chanel suits in mint condition, Le Smoking jackets and trousers by Yves Saint Laurent, Haute Couture Lanvin black-tie gowns from the 1930s, and mod Pierre Cardin minidresses. Owner William Banks-Blaney, an expert on the history of designer clothing, has an exceptionally discerning eye—and myriad sources—so everything here is as wearable as it is collectible. Accordingly, the prices are on the high side, but the quality is exceptional.

2 MARYLEBONE STREET . W1G 8JQ 🚇 GREAT PORTLAND STREET/BOND STREET
☎ 020 7487 4322 🌐 WILLIAMVINTAGE.COM

Merchant Archive

Merchant Archive's crisp women's clothing—bold but not overly showy print tops, elegantly draped silk blouses, understated but modern cocktail dresses—has a classic sensibility reflective of store owner Sophie Merchant's roots in selling vintage wear. The confident pieces she creates are popular with the neighborhood's stylish residents along with quite a few British fashion editors. The shop features a concise selection of Merchant-designed handbags with a timeless bent as well as a choice of a few readily giftable home goods, such as ceramic serving bowls finished with a matte gray glaze and chunky handmade glass tumblers.

19 KENSINGTON PARK ROAD . W11 2EU ☎ LADBROKE GROVE/NOTTING GILL GATE
☎ 020 7229 9006 ⊕ MERCHANTARCHIVE.COM

Luna & Curious

There's a little bit of everything at this amiable Shoreditch boutique: jewelry, clothing, pottery, kids' woolen hats and mufflers, greeting cards, gift books, striped socks, Swedish musk soap, and glittery nail polish. Somehow the mix works seamlessly, making the shop an ideal spot for browsing as well as gift hunting. Of particular note are the traditional bone china cups and plates with a playful twist, such as detailed drawings of dogs, patterns from Japanese kimonos, and geometric patterns that are as pretty to display as to liven up a cup of tea or coffee.

24–26 CALVERT AVENUE . E2 7JP 🚇 OLD STREET/LIVERPOOL STREET; SHOREDITCH HIGH STREET
☎ 020 3222 0034 ⊕ LUNAANDCURIOUS.COM

The Vintage Showroom

The name says it all: this Covent Garden spot is packed with used men's clothing, shoes, and accessories from many eras—with rack upon rack to plow through at leisure. The shop is an excellent source for outerwear, such as military parkas with fur trim and hefty leather military jackets, as well as decades-old blazers and button-down shirts that still look crisp. Co-owners Douglas Gunn and Roy Luckett also operate an appointment-only studio filled with still more vintage pieces for men on Conlan Street in Notting Hill; at that location, designers and stylists come in for inspiration, but the clothing isn't typically for sale.

14 EARLHAM STREET . WC2H 9LN ☎ COVENT GARDEN/LEICESTER SQUARE

☎ 020 7836 3964 ⊕ THEVINTAGESHOWROOM.COM

Rachel Entwistle
Store & Studio

The edgy, tribal-inspired gold and silver creations that jeweler Rachel Entwistle sells in her Shoreditch boutique are indisputably au courant—a perfect fit for the hipster district. The rings are often bold conversation starters, including one fashioned from metal loops shaped and carved to resemble slithering snakes, to wear alone or stacked in combination; eyes crafted from tiny emeralds or rubies are optional. There are also small items for impulse purchases, such as silver stud earrings that can be bought as uniform pairs, intentionally mismatched, or alone; prices across the board are, in keeping with the neighborhood, unintimidating.

5A CLUB ROW . E1 6JX 🚇 LIVERPOOL STREET/BETHNAL GREEN ROAD; SHOREDITCH HIGH STREET
☎ 020 3566 8777 ⊕ RACHELENTWISTLE.CO.UK

Stowers Bespoke

Savile Row is, for many men, synonymous with classically tailored suits of the finest quality. The street is filled with traditional clothiers along those lines, including Anderson & Sheppard and Gieves & Hawkes. Stowers Bespoke uses centuries-old techniques to craft its custom suits, but its pieces are the opposite of stuffy or standard. With a moneyed clientele that includes international royalty and powerful businessmen, Stowers uses offbeat, bold fabrics and brash linings to transform each suit into something that's truly unique and frequently quite flamboyant. Despite the bravado of some of the shop's suiting materials, the hand-sewn quality of its pieces is irrefutably high.

13 SAVILE ROW . W1S 3NE 🚇 GREEN PARK/PICCADILLY CIRCUS ☎ 020 7287 3080
🌐 STOWERS.LONDON

Hub Shop

This pair of shops—one stocks menswear; the other, women's clothing and accessories—sells unassuming yet fashionable items for everyday wear: Stutterheim rain parkas, striped cotton Petit Bateau tees, Grenson brogues, and needle cord button-down shirts from the London-based manufacturer Folk. In keeping with the not-overly-fancy aesthetic, nothing's too expensive and the colors tend toward neutrals—black, gray, and white. There is another Hub Store that stocks items for both sexes at 2a Ada Street, off Broadway Market.

MEN'S: 88 STOKE NEWINGTON CHURCH STREET . N16 0AP ☎ 020 7275 8160
WOMEN'S: 49 STOKE NEWINGTON CHURCH STREET . N16 0AR ☎ 020 7254 4494
STOKE NEWINGTON ⊕ HUBSHOP.CO.UK

BEAUTY, GROOMING, AND WELLNESS

Twiggy's false eyelashes and pale lips; Amy Winehouse's bouffant; David Bowie's bold and ever-changing makeup and spiked orange circa-Ziggy coif: in the case of some London-born icons, their beauty and grooming styles are an immutable part of their internationally known images. Beautifiers—both products to use at home and indulgent spa and salon treatments—are intensely popular with less renowned Londoners, too. The most impressive places offer something special—custom-blended fragrances, nuanced hair coloring, a perfectly painted manicure—and their staffs can knowledgably tackle any issue, whether it's help with choosing a face mask or kneading out stress. London also has a long tradition of top-notch homeopathic and alternative therapies; the purveyors of these remedies and services began offering them way before nonmedical methods of wellness were trendy or mainstream.

Penhaligon's

William Penhaligon, the founder of this iconic perfumer, created his first fragrance in the 1870s; his eponymous company is still thriving today and is the holder of two Royal Warrants, the official notice that confirms that a brand is used by the British monarchy. The company's heritage scents, such as the citrusy Blenheim Bouquet and amber-and-sandalwood-based Hammam Bouquet, are as resonant now as they were when they were originally introduced; recent additions to the collection are built around more feminine notes such as orange blossom and lily of the valley. Although there are a handful of Penhaligon locations in London, shopping on Wellington Street suggests the grandeur of another era, as does the packaging, which includes chunky glass bottles labeled with old-fashioned typography and decorated with brightly colored grosgrain ribbons.

41 WELLINGTON STREET . WC2E 7BN 🚇 COVENT GARDEN/TEMPLE ☎ 020 7240 6256
🌐 PENHALIGONS.COM

Barber Streisand
Unisex Barbers

The antithesis of an intimidating, trend-obsessed hair salon, this extra-friendly hairdresser attracts a loyal following of people who live and work in the neighborhood as well as students from nearby schools such as City University London, who are offered a healthy discount. Although the salon doesn't take itself too seriously—starting, of course, with its clever name, once tweeted in approval by the singer herself—the haircuts here are top-notch. On weekends, there can be a long wait, but no one seems to mind, as it's surrounded by a large handful of appealing boutiques and cafés that make killing a bit of time pre-trim a pleasure.

45 EXMOUTH MARKET . EC1R 4QL 🚇 ANGEL/FARRINGDON ☎ 020 7278 6524
🌐 BARBERSTREISAND.COM

Neal's Yard Remedies

The original location and namesake of the wellness brand that is now known as Neal's Yard Remedies, with branches throughout London and Great Britain, was 15 Neal's Yard, a shop located in a small alcove in Covent Garden. Treatments including reflexology, acupuncture, and Indian head massage are still offered there, and today, a few doors away, a second shop is stocked with a line of organic skincare products, naturally scented with ingredients such as English lavender, ylang ylang, and frankincense and bottled in trademark cobalt blue packaging. There are also natural unguents and balms to soothe issues such as eczema and diaper rash. The seasoned staff is well equipped to advise on the best products for your skin type.

2 AND 15 NEAL'S YARD . WC2H 9DP 🚇 COVENT GARDEN/LEICESTER SQUARE
☎ 020 7379 7662; 020 7379 7222 ⊕ NEALSYARDREMEDIES.COM

TINCTURE BAR
Bespoke herbal blends, for your wellbeing

NATURA

Perfumer H

Lyn Harris—the "H" in Perfumer H—is the founder of the popular fragrance line Miller Harris, best known for its wearable unisex scents such as Citron Citron and Tangerine Vert. Her latest venture is headquartered in a comfortable boutique on a sedate Marylebone street, where the sensibility is relaxed and anti-hard-sell; shoppers are encouraged to linger, sometimes over a cup of Earl Grey tea. Here, costly custom-created fragrances take center stage; they are blended in the lab in back by a professional perfumer. Nonetheless, there is always a seasonal selection of more affordable but equally nuanced premade perfumes available, as well as richly scented candles in fragrances including fresh ivy and rich, evocative smoke.

106A CRAWFORD STREET . W1H 2HZ 🚇 BAKER STREET/MARYLEBONE ☎ 020 7258 7859
🌐 PERFUMERH.COM

Cowshed

This small chain of comfy and casual spas is an offshoot of the members' club Soho House, which also carries its unisex range of products with witty names, such as Lazy Cow, a blend of jasmine and chamomile that adds a feeling of calm to shower gel and moisturizing lotion. This cozy location, which also serves lattes and light dishes from a café menu, has become an anchor of the charming, upscale Primrose Hill. Weekdays the folksy space gets busy with neighborhood moms popping in for precise pedicures as they lounge on one of its oversized leather upholstered chairs. On weekends, after a facial or massage in one of the treatment rooms downstairs, patrons often opt for brunch, lingering over avocado toast with poached eggs and smoothies.

115–117 REGENT'S PARK ROAD . NW1 8UR 🚇 CHALK FARM ☎ 020 3725 2777
🌐 COWSHEDONLINE.COM/PRIMROSEHILL

BLUE MALLOW CHAMOMILE ORANGE

DR LEAVER'S BRONCHIAL LOZENGES

SULPHO

G. Baldwin & Co

Since 1844, Baldwins, as the loyal clientele calls this well-stocked store, has been selling herbal, homeopathic, and natural remedies to the Elephant and Castle community. The extensive selection in the main shop includes teas, vitamins, herbs, and tinctures, while the space next door is dedicated to healthy food, from nuts and porridge for the pantry to freshly baked bread and refrigerated smoothies to go. The vibe is very friendly: customers, plenty of whom the helpful staff know by name, tend to linger and chat.

171–173 WALWORTH ROAD . SE17 1RW ⚲ ELEPHANT & CASTLE/KENSINGTON ☎ 020 7703 5550
🌐 BALDWINS.CO.UK

D. R. Harris & Co. Ltd.

This heritage business has been selling grooming products in the posh, centrally located St. James's since 1790. The packaging of many of the brand's sophisticated products—sturdy glass bottles and ceramic tubs affixed with antique-style paper labels—harks back to its early days. Some of the most striking fragrances sold here, imbued with lavender, lime, and herbs, recall that era, too. Particularly popular are the men's items, including badger-bristled shaving brushes, leather dopp kits packed with horn combs and a shoe horn, and formidable pottery vessels for toothbrushes and bars of soap. In the back is a quiet working pharmacy, which just might be the most stylish spot in town to pick up a prescription. There is also a sister location, without an apothecary, around the corner at 52 Piccadilly.

29 ST. JAMES'S STREET . SW1A 1BH   GREEN PARK   ☎ 020 7930 3915
⊕ DRHARRIS.CO.UK

Floris

Fans of this heritage perfumery, open since 1730, have included the likes of Florence Nightingale and Winston Churchill, the latter of whom had a soft spot for the lavender-laced Special No.12 and Stephanotis. Both scents are still available today, along with more recent introductions such as the heady Honey Oud as well as scented candles, room sprays, soaps, and other toiletries. There's a selection of many types of scents—woody, floral, oriental, citrus—with the additional and more expensive option of working with the store to create a custom-designed fragrance. The brand is still family owned, and the perfumes are made in Devon, a few hours away. In addition to this evocative flagship store, there is a second London Floris location in Belgravia at 147 Ebury Street.

89 JERMYN STREET . SW1Y 6JH 🚇 GREEN PARK/PICCADILLY CIRCUS ☎ 020 7930 2885
🌐 FLORISLONDON.COM

Jo Loves

Jo Malone, founder of the distinctive collection of indulgent scented products that bear her name, opened this welcoming boutique to showcase her latest venture, Jo Loves, a line of lovely scents inspired by memories and things she loves. The fragrances—some of which are based on unexpected notes such as truffle, coriander, and sweet pea—are unisex and packaged in streamlined bottles that are at once modern and reminiscent of art deco geometry. Shopping for fragrances here is a leisurely and pleasurable experience, thanks to help from a buoyant staff who take ample time helping customers test scents on a wide worktop that's more suggestive of a cocktail bar than a fragrance counter. Beautifully scented candles are on offer as well as companion lotions and scented bath products.

42 ELIZABETH STREET . SW1W 9NZ 🚇 SLOANE SQUARE ☎ 020 7730 6091

🌐 JOLOVES.COM

John Bell & Croyden

In business in various locations since 1798 and with a loyal clientele that includes the royal family, this beloved London chemist has an allure that makes buying aspirin or vitamins feel like a designer purchase. Some of that glamour comes down to the prowess of the staff, who is always available to help and advise, and some of it is related to the design of the expansive shop itself, as the space is more akin to that of a fine department store than the usual local neighborhood retail chain. The selection is comprehensive; it includes homeopathic remedies and imported goods from all over the world as well as mainstream medicines, cosmetics, and grooming supplies.

50–54 WIGMORE STREET . W1U 2AU 🚇 BOND STREET ☎ 020 7935 5555
🌐 JOHNBELLCROYDEN.CO.UK

Josh Wood Colour

This salon on a quiet little street in affluent Holland Park is the hair salon of choice for stylish women from all over London. As the salon's name implies, color is the star here. Wood, who is well known in Britain, built his reputation on dyeing the locks of celebrities and models, but the salon also offers first-rate haircuts and blowouts. Beyond the services, the unconventional accoutrements in the space—iPads with customized playlists, fresh flower arrangements, and tasty snacks and smoothies to enjoy during services—make the experience of getting a treatment here as outstanding as the results.

6 LANSDOWNE MEWS . W11 3AN 🚇 HOLLAND PARK ☎ 020 3393 0977
🌐 JOSHWOODCOLOUR.COM

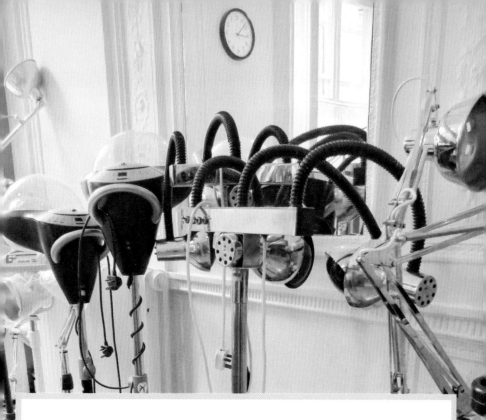

Philip Kingsley
Trichological Clinic

Tucked in a quiet, posh residential side street a few blocks from Selfridges, this acclaimed British salon has been helping women and men with problematic hair since 1968. Except for the setting, the service might not sound glamorous, but the Kingsley staff is so gentle and experienced, they somehow make dealing with thinning hair or flaky dandruff feel like a spa experience. It is a hair salon—with a large upstairs treatment room filled with retro-inspired hair dryers and stylist stations—but, unlike a typical place specializing in cuts and color, initial appointments begin with a long consultation in a private, antique-furnished room to diagnose issues and treatment. The clinic is not medical, but it does offer decades of know-how on improving the health and feel of the hair and scalp. Even without an appointment, you can stop in to buy one of the clinic's effective range of at-home products, including Elasticizer, an intensive conditioner that was originally created for Audrey Hepburn in the 1970s.

54 GREEN STREET . W1K 6RU ⚇ MARBLE ARCH/BOND STREET ☎ 020 7629 4004
⊕ PHILIPKINGSLEY.CO.UK

DECOR, FLOWERS, AND ITEMS FOR THE HOME

For some, imagining best-in-class British decorative items brings to mind antique bone china teacups and ornate chintz wallpaper. But the city's array of retailers specializing in items for the home—including stationery, lighting, tabletop gifts, and contemporary furniture—offers a varied mix of styles and sensibilities that goes well beyond a traditional aesthetic. It's easy to find, for example, ultramodern kitchen utensils, handcrafted pottery, centuries-old antiques, and letterpress greeting cards for sale, all within a relatively short distance of one another. There are also numerous independently owned boutiques that focus on a specific—and sometimes quirky—item or category of items such as vinyl records, hand-cast bells, imported loose tea, even deeply fragrant candles. All are compelling destinations in which to browse, even if you leave without a purchase.

Scarlet & Violet

Unpretentious, vibrant, relaxed, and quaint—just like the northwest London community of Kensal Green, where it is located—this popular florist has been a local favorite for nearly a decade. Owner Vic Brotherson and her team create lavish arrangements, often using unexpected vessels, such as vintage enamelware jugs, for an effect that's homey, intentionally not too polished, and with a slightly rustic charm. Wedding bouquets are one of Scarlet & Violet's strengths; supermodel Kate Moss famously walked down the aisle holding an assembly of lilies with pale pink and ivory roses that the florists created for her.

76 CHAMBERLAYNE ROAD . NW10 3JJ 🚇 KENSAL GREEN; KENSAL GREEN
☎ 020 8969 9446 🌐 SCARLETANDVIOLET.COM

Postcard Teas

It's hard to imagine a location more central than Postcard Teas' inviting space on Dering Street—just off Bond Street and only a few minutes from busy Oxford Street—but many people, even lifelong Londoners, aren't aware of this jewel of a tea shop. The tea on offer is of impeccable quality, grown on small Asian farms that prioritize excellence over volume. The green teas are utterly impressive—including longjing (Dragon Well) tea from Hangzhou, China, and richly herbaceous sencha grown on Mount Fuji—but the ultimate standout might just be the Earl Grey, made with cold-pressed Calabrian bergamot oil for a more citrusy punch than the variety typically delivers. All the tea is packaged in beautiful, art-adorned canisters, and the infectiously tea-obsessed staff is happy to offer detailed guidance to help you make the perfect choice.

9 DERING STREET . W1S 1AG 🚇 BOND STREET ☎ 020 7629 3654
🌐 POSTCARDTEAS.COM

Fee Fee La Fou HQ

With an exterior that's painted with a bubble-gum-pink store logo and bright peppermint stripes, it's apparent that Fee Fee La Fou HQ isn't a run-of-the-mill gift store. The brainchild of the artist Fiona Duffelen, whose work has appeared in prestigious arenas including the Royal College of Art, the shop specializes in carrying innovative, relatively affordable handmade items by painters, jewelry makers, and sculptors. Nonetheless, the vibe is fun rather than highbrow. Standouts include spunky Perspex necklaces, milk jugs decorated with ornate skulls or giant flamingoes, and colorful throw pillows with patchwork images of classic cartoon characters that will add a dash of pop art–inspired color to a child's room. Well-designed greeting cards, gift wrap, and streamlined leather pencil cases round out the boutique's eclectic mix.

6 BRADBURY STREET . N16 8JN 🚇 DALSTON KINGSLAND ☎ 020 7249 1238
🌐 FEEFEELAFOUENTERPRISES.COM

Whitechapel Bell Foundry

This fully operational bell-making facility has been in business for more than four hundred years—since 1570, to be exact. The Liberty Bell and the bells that ring in Big Ben were all made on these premises. But visiting this unique heritage establishment is more than just revisiting a piece of history; it's a place to see expert craftsmen, using centuries-old techniques, cast the hefty brass bells by hand. To do that, it's necessary to book a spot on one of the foundry's workshop tours, which are held a couple times a month and fill up quickly. Every day, Whitechapel is a resource for truly unique handcrafted gifts: shiny hand bells with hand-turned hardwood handles, hefty steel and brass door knockers, and the type of tabletop bell that would've been used to ring for one's butler a hundred years ago. Also available are minibells, with a diameter of about two inches, which make an attractive desk ornament, especially when engraved with a monogram or significant date.

32–34 WHITECHAPEL ROAD . E1 1DY 🚇 ALDGATE EAST ☎ 020 7247 2599
🌐 WHITECHAPELBELLFOUNDRY.CO.UK

Pentreath & Hall

Ben Pentreath, who co-owns this Bloomsbury shop with Bridie Hall, has designed interiors for a range of clients, from trendsetters and Hollywood celebrities to the royal family. The shop sells a handpicked selection of salient home goods, both vintage and new, some designed by Hall. The hard-to-resist array includes muted woven Catalan linen napkins, Astier de Villatte plates, antique framed prints, bright African baskets, and lacquered crystal tumblers inlaid with gold letters for impromptu monogrammed gifts. This is the type of store that's worth a stop for design inspiration as much as for bona fide shopping, although leaving without even a small purchase, such as a hand-bound journal covered in patterned cloth, is a challenge because the offerings are all so appealing.

17 RUGBY ST . WC1N 3QT 🚇 RUSSELL SQUARE/HOLBORN/CHANCERY LANE ☎ 020 7430 2526
🌐 PENTREATH-HALL.COM

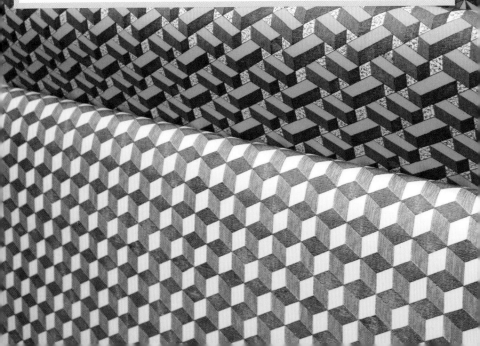

Issue 7 — Asparagus Fern
A curious observer of ordinary plants and other greenery
Ugly on the inside

PAUL WILLIAMS

Grace & Thorn

This creative florist is where in-the-know East Enders—as well as style-centric businesses such as Burberry, Christopher Kane, and Dover Street Market—go for beautiful, effulgent arrangements throughout the week, even on Sundays, when Columbia Road's crowded flower market opens up just a few minutes' walk away. Owner Nik Southern and her team make a priority of using seasonal flowers in their arrangements, although they specialize in gorgeous rose presentations that are always lovely without ever looking too formal or overdone. The florist also regularly holds flower-arranging and floral crown–making workshops. There is a second Grace & Thorn shop in Soho at 7 Greens Court, just off Brewer Street.

338 HACKNEY ROAD . E2 7AX 🚇 BETHNAL GREEN; HOXTON ☎ 020 7739 1521, EXT. 1
🌐 GRACEANDTHORN.COM

Labour and Wait

At this popular Shoreditch store, cofounders and former menswear designers Rachel Wythe-Moran and Simon Watkins carry a personally selected and highly curated selection of utilitarian items of good design, which makes this a perfect spot to shop for stylish, affordable small gift items. The merchandise reflects a deep respect for tradition, from the old-school glossy Brown Betty teapots that have been used in British homes for many generations to striped cotton Breton shirts from France. Some of the goods are a bit quirky—such as boxy plastic totes from Sweden that can be used either to store magazines at home or to carry groceries; home items have special priority. Other highlights of the selection include soap flakes from Marseille, German pocket fountain pens and colored chalk, Portuguese toothpaste, and Dutch bicycle repair kits.

85 REDCHURCH STREET . E2 7DJ 🚇 LIVERPOOL STREET/BETHNAL GREEN; SHOREDITCH HIGH STREET ☎ 020 7729 6253 ⊕ LABOURANDWAIT.CO.UK

The Old Cinema

Housed in a former movie theater, this massive vintage furniture store feels somewhat like an indoor flea market, with room after room stocked with an eccentric yet appealing array of home goods: midcentury chairs, toys from the 1950s, old advertising signs, traditional leather sofas, angular desk lamps, and framed rock concert posters. On weekends, it's a favorite place for the neighborhood's laid-back but stylish residents—often fueled by a flat white or banana-and-peanut-butter smoothie from High Road House, the hotel and brasserie next door—to source both furnishings and design inspiration. On weekdays, interior decorators abound, hunting for finds for their clients. Although it's a cavernous space, the shop gets crowded, so the best strategy is to come early, regardless of the day.

160 CHISWICK HIGH ROAD . W4 1PR 🚇 TURNHAM GREEN ☎ 020 8995 4166

🌐 THEOLDCINEMA.CO.UK

Comfort Station

Designed and made on the premises by shop owner Amy Anderson, the jewelry at Comfort Station has a unique, attention-getting, but not overly bold aesthetic. The best pieces are architectural in feel, including hefty hexagon-shaped stacking rings and oversized hoop earrings that hang from a thin bar. Anderson crafts her pieces in sterling silver or gold plate and the quality is high, yet the prices are extremely fair. Comfort Station's decor is as engaging as the jewelry; vintage suitcases are mounted on the wall and used as display cabinets; antique books are mounted open and in groupings on the wall and adorned with Anderson's pieces. Also for sale are bone china mugs covered in ornate hand-drawn illustrations and finished with twenty-two-carat-gold detailing that makes them feel more like art than a receptacle for tea or coffee.

22 CHESHIRE STREET . E2 6EH 🚇 LIVERPOOL STREET; SHOREDITCH HIGH STREET
☎ 020 7033 9099 ⊕ COMFORTSTATION.CO.UK

Summerill & Bishop

Located on a bright corner in Holland Park, this well-stocked boutique carries best-in-class versions of kitchen essentials, many of which are sourced from hard-to-find, long-established manufacturers in continental Europe. Included in the array are sleek Laguiole knives, hand-printed linen napkins by Bertozzi, Paderno pans, and Peugeot Paris pepper mills. Co-owners June Summerill and Bernadette Bishop also scour flea markets throughout France for vintage finds, such as Bakelite-handled eggbeaters and pale blue linen napkins, to sell alongside the new items, which are as attractive and well designed as they are functional.

100 PORTLAND ROAD . W11 4LQ 🚊 HOLLAND PARK/LADBROKE GROVE ☎ 020 7229 1337
🌐 SUMMERILLANDBISHOP.COM

KITCHENWARE

DOWNSTAIRS

The Monocle Shop

Founded by the journalist Tyler Brûlé, the monthly magazine *Monocle* is known for showcasing practical, well-designed items that are stylish in a quiet way, among its diverse editorial features. This compact boutique sells those items, the bulk of which are collaborations between Monocle and other companies that share its level of taste. These include zip cases for money or electronics made by Japan's Delfonics, long woven angora scarves created for the brand by Scotland's Begg & Co., and candles designed by Comme des Garçons that are infused with Monocle-branded scents. Although the publication operates boutiques in New York, Hong Kong, and Toronto, the London shop near the main office was its first and best captures its discerning aesthetic.

2A GEORGE STREET . W1U 3QS 🚇 BOND STREET/BAKER STREET ☎ 020 7486 8770
🌐 MONOCLE.COM

The Monocle Café

A few minutes from its shop on George Street, Monocle operates this café, the stylish neighborhood's de facto canteen for well-prepared Allpress coffee, fresh mint tea, macarons, and carrot cake, among a short list of other items to go. There's also an eclectic international menu of heartier dishes such as Japanese chicken udon soup paired with a shrimp katsu sandwich, Scandinavian breakfast with smoked salmon, and quinoa salad with grilled Greek halloumi cheese. To enjoy these dishes, most customers linger in the snug room behind the take-out area outfitted with comfortable seating, a few unusual knickknacks, and a large-screen TV broadcasting short films on tastemaker destinations and noteworthy entrepreneurs that are produced by, yes, the folks at Monocle. The company also has a café that sells hundreds of magazines and newspaper titles as well as hot drinks and pastries called Kioskafe at 31 Norfolk Place near Paddington Station.

18 CHILTERN STREET . W1U 7QA ⛿ BOND STREET/BAKER STREET ☎ 020 7135 2040
🌐 CAFE.MONOCLE.COM

twentytwentyone

Strictly speaking, twentytwentyone is a furniture store—albeit one with an extremely high style quotient—but there are so many attractive small items for sale, it's easy to forget that the shop is really known for its streamlined sofas and sculptural overhead lighting fixtures. Located on a quiet street in Islington, the boutique attracts mostly locals, interior decorators, and design aficionados. On the main floor, a carefully chosen selection of gifts and home accessories—German Kaweco fountain pens, curved Georg Jensen water pitchers, streamlined white vases by Lyngby Porcelain, scented candles adorned with illustrations by Fornasetti—make the shop a wonderful place in which to browse or pick up gifts. On the lower level, there are furnishings by renowned icons such as Charles and Ray Eames and Mies van der Rohe as well as pieces that are made in-house from designs by more insider midcentury names such as Robin Day and William Plunkett. All can be shipped internationally. There is also a twentytwentyone showroom a fifteen-minute walk away, not far from Sadler's Wells Theatre, at 18c River Street.

274–275 UPPER STREET . N1 2UA 🚇 ANGEL/HIGHBURY & ISLINGTON
☎ 020 7288 1996 🌐 TWENTYTWENTYONE.COM

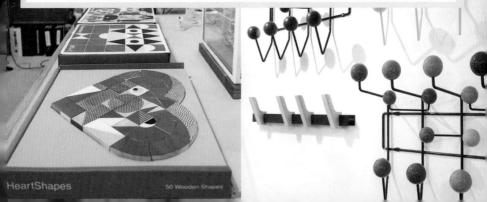

LASSCO Ropewalk

LASSCO, officially known as the London Architectural Salvage and Supply Company, is a gigantic emporium and an extraordinary resource for both decorators and furniture lovers, thanks to its wide selection of unusual and authentic period fireplaces, doors, iron fixtures, ornate chandeliers, metal garden ornaments, sinks, and ceramic taps. The store's always busy on Saturdays—when the lively Maltby Street food market is held right outside—but the space is vast enough to accommodate the crowds. The savviest shoppers come on weekdays, when it's less of a scene. Even if buying large-size home furnishings isn't in your plans, LASSCO is worth a visit if you have an interest in antique furniture and oddities or if you're just looking for design inspiration. There are also LASSCO locations at 30 Wandsworth Road in Vauxhall and in Oxfordshire, but this shop, near other neighborhood destinations such as the Fashion and Textile Museum (page 22) and White Cube (page 27), is the most popular.

41 MALTBY STREET . SE1 3PA ☗ BERMONDSEY ☎ 020 7394 8061
🌐 LASSCO.CO.UK

The Lacquer Chest

Kensington Church Street, with its cluster of stores specializing in vintage items from the last couple of centuries, is a haven for antique lovers. One of the shops, the Lacquer Chest, offers an enchanting and diverse selection of handpicked items, among them floral-patterned nineteenth-century ceramics, small marble sculptures, Windsor chairs, glass apothecary bottles, and vintage nightstand lamps on its ground floor.

75 KENSINGTON CHURCH STREET . W8 4BG 🚇 HIGH STREET KENSINGTON/NOTTING HILL GATE
☎ 020 7937 1306 🌐 LACQUERCHEST.COM

House of Voltaire

Studio Voltaire is a nonprofit gallery that hosts a range of art exhibitions and performances in a former church with a vaulted ceiling. House of Voltaire, its retail arm, carries items produced by artists who are clever, eclectic, and unusual, such as Jeremy Deller's sturdy black canvas tote bag adorned with the phrase "God Bless David Bowie." Also here: boldly printed beach towels by Louise Gray and Ella Kruglyanskaya that you'll want to frame rather than use, towels by the designer Peter Saville, and commissioned etchings and prints by artists such as Pablo Bronstein and Sol Calero. Although Clapham isn't on most visitors' itineraries, make the trip: the pieces here are worth it. Getting here is easy via the Tube, and the stop is not all that far from either Victoria or Waterloo Station.

1A NELSON'S ROW . SW4 7JR 🚇 CLAPHAM COMMON ☎ 020 7622 1294
🌐 STUDIOVOLTAIRE.ORG

Another Country

Much of the sleek wooden furniture sold at this Marylebone retailer—started by Paul de Zwart, also the cofounder of *Wallpaper* magazine—is understated and stylish, suggestive of classic Japanese or Scandinavian design in its minimalism and clean lines. Many of the larger pieces are British-made, and the shop will ship pieces worldwide if you just can't resist buying them. You'll also find unusual interpretations of standard home accessories, such as sculptural brass bookends designed by the Bauhaus artist Carl Auböck II and contoured Palutta wooden bowls and serving ware coated with smooth Japanese lacquer. Also of note is the store's well-priced line of streamlined desk essentials in maple and walnut, including a tape holder and pencil cup that make even the messiest workspace look smart.

8 CRAWFORD STREET . W1H 1BT 🚇 MARYLEBONE/BAKER STREET ☎ 020 7486 3251
🌐 ANOTHERCOUNTRY.COM

After Noah

In its early days, this split-level Islington store specialized in selling vintage furniture and restoring old pieces and flea market finds. Though that side of the business still thrives and is now located on the shop's basement floor, the ground floor is now essentially a modern curio shop that the neighborhood's discerning residents rely on for unusual tabletop items and gifts. Some of what's here consists of decorative new conversation starters—including bronze-coated skeletons and a sculpted resin bear's head to hang in lieu of actual taxidermy—although there are many appealing items that make less of a statement, such as a heavy brass hourglass and world globes inspired by antique models. Located in a family-oriented community, the shop offers an excellent toy selection based on traditional childhood pleasures, such as dolls and arts and crafts, rather than technology- and electronics-oriented gadgets.

121 UPPER STREET . N1 1QP 🚇 ANGEL/HIGHBURY & ISLINGTON ☎ 020 7359 4281
🌐 AFTERNOAH.COM

STATIONERY, BOOKS, AND GIFTS

Arguably Europe's most modern city, London is still a place where traditional practices are proudly upheld, from writing thank-you notes by hand on engraved stationery to reading a beautiful hardbound first edition of a classic novel. The best stores that carry stationery, books, and other specialty items—from a handmade umbrella with a wood frame to a twelve-inch vinyl album by an up-and-coming rock band on a Shoreditch-based record label—are, more often than not, independently owned, singular in nature, and situated in vibrant residential communities, away from the tourist trail.

Daunt Books

With its dark oak detailing and rows of hardback-filled shelves, Daunt Books is the epitome of a classic, well-appointed bookshop—a thriving destination that draws in book lovers from the moment its doors open in the morning until it closes at night. The approachable staff are book lovers eager to help with suggestions, so it's not surprising that those who venture in rarely leave without a new book tucked inside one of the store's logoed bags. There are other Daunt branches peppered around the city, but the original shop on Marylebone High Street is the most charming.

83 MARYLEBONE HIGH STREET . W1U 4QW ☗ BAKER STREET/BOND STREET ☎ 020 7224 2295
⊕ DAUNTBOOKS.CO.UK/SHOPS/MARYLEBONE

Hoxton Street Monster Supplies

Cofounded by the author Nick Hornby, this appealing emporium of what it calls "Bespoke and Everyday Items for the Living, Dead, and Undead" donates its profits to a neighborhood tutoring program that helps kids improve their writing. The shop sells an array of sweets, packaged for monsters of all ages, such as cubed ear wax (delectable bite-size pieces of cream fudge) and its Tinned Fear series, each can of which, from Escalating Panic to Mortal Fear, offers individually wrapped candy and a specially commissioned short story by a writer of note, such as Zadie Smith. The shop also sells other small monster-themed gift items such as Fang Floss (twine), Moonlight (a flashlight), and assorted salts harvested in Wales by Halen Môn and enhanced with a variety of flavors, such as Salt Made of Tears of Envy, which contains celery, making it an excellent ingredient for a terrifyingly good Bloody Mary.

159 HOXTON STREET . N1 6PJ 🚇 OLD STREET; HOXTON ☎ 020 7729 4159
🌐 MONSTERSUPPLIES.ORG

Hoxton Street Monster Supplies
ESTD 1818
~ Purveyor of Quality Goods for Monsters of Every Kind ~

GUTS & GARLIC CHUTNEY

the day of spilling, our guts chutney is
plement to body-temperature meats
suitable for vampires.

CHALICE

Hoxton Street Monster Supplies

ESTᴰ 1818

~ Purveyor of Quality Goods for Monsters of Every Kind ~

FRESH FARTS

The concentrated stench of fear: quite the finest delicacy for any discerning monster. These ghastly gaseous excretions are gathered freshly by our lackeys each night; and are universally acknowledged to be the most pungent in the land.

Present and Correct

On a quiet street near Sadler's Wells Theatre and an easy walk from Angel Station and Exmouth Market, this compact store carries stationery, writing instruments, and office and school supplies, all curated deftly and precisely by its founder, the graphic designer Neal Whittington. The store has a decidedly retro vibe, underscored by the wide range of vintage items for sale, including 1950s address labels from France, 1960s airmail correspondence kits, and postage stamps from around the world. There are plenty of new items here too, although they share the aesthetic, from trim Japanese Penco notebooks to adhesive tape made of real wood that you can write on. The store's crisp, pristine displays are artful and, for lovers of stationery and striking design, irresistible. Since everything is small and not very expensive, Present and Correct is a wonderful source of unique souvenirs and gifts.

23 ARLINGTON WAY . EC1R 1UY 🚇 ANGEL ☎ 020 7278 2460
🌐 PRESENTANDCORRECT.COM

Lutyens & Rubinstein Bookshop

A true haven for book lovers, this welcoming duplex in Notting Hill—a high-ceilinged space stuffed with volumes lined up on black wooden shelving—houses both a bookshop and a literary agency. The shop is on the small side, and the selection, though sized accordingly, is extremely well curated, from novels and biographies to large coffee-table books. Browsing and lingering are encouraged—regulars often grab a cup of tea or coffee from downstairs when they stop by. It's also a popular neighborhood place to pick up letterpress greeting cards or pretty paperweights by one of Lutyens' literary agents, Jane Finigan, who has created them exclusively for the store since it opened. The shop also offers subscription programs for readers of all ages, essentially a "book of the month" club in which titles are custom chosen for clients and sent to them by mail; for kids receiving their shipments at home or boarding school, a tiny sweet treat is included for added enjoyment.

21 KENSINGTON PARK ROAD . W11 2EU 🚇 NOTTING HILL GATE ☎ 020 7229 1010
🌐 LUTYENSRUBINSTEIN.CO.UK

Heywood Hill

Since opening in 1936, this refined Mayfair bookshop has catered to an illustrious clientele in the neighborhood and beyond, including Queen Elizabeth II, who has her orders shipped to Buckingham Palace, and the mystery author John le Carré, who used the store as a location in his book *Tinker Tailor Soldier Spy*. Although the bookstore is situated in an elite neighborhood, the atmosphere is warm and the staff is accommodating and happy to assist, whether you're looking for a new best seller or an obscure old tome. The space isn't huge but is overly packed with books: weighing down round tables in the center of the store, stuffing the simple shelving that lines the molding-topped walls, filling an antique glass-fronted wooden vitrine in the front with collectible volumes, and sometimes stacked on the plush wall-to-wall carpet. The store carries an impressive selection of new titles and also offers a selection of vintage leather-bound books and first editions in a wide range of categories. Down a narrow staircase is a well-chosen selection of books for children from babies to teens that includes both new releases and time-honored classics; they are displayed in a charming nook that lends itself to younger children, who frequently linger with their parents for some prepurchase storytime.

10 CURZON STREET . W1J 5HH 🚇 GREEN PARK ☎ 020 7629 0647

🌐 HEYWOODHILL.COM

Smythson of Bond Street

Smythson's engraved stationery and distinctively textured leather-bound diaries have been the choice of both royalty and well-to-do civilians for more than 125 years; these days, the brand also offers precisely crafted handbags, briefcases, and cases for cell phones and other gadgets. This huge flagship store—with its rotating display of museum-quality pieces from its archives—gives a sense of the brand as well as its blend of heritage and modern practicality. An on-site engraver can add initials in a choice of typefaces and sizes for most leather items while you wait. Personalized stationery, which can include one of Smythson's lovely illustrated motifs as well as the requisite name and address, takes longer but can be shipped worldwide.

40 NEW BOND STREET . W1S 2DE 🚇 BOND STREET/GREEN PARK

☎ 020 7629 8558 🌐 SMYTHSON.COM

Sautter Cigars

Sautter Cigars is, at its core, a specialist store in which to buy high-end cigars from respected Cuban brands such as Partagas and Cohiba, although it would be easy to mistake it for one of London's fabled private clubs, since there are always a few regulars sitting on a row of chairs chatting animatedly while puffing a new purchase at leisure. The engaging atmosphere has attracted shoppers for more than fifty years, well before its Mount Street location was surrounded by trend-conscious designer stores such as Céline, Lanvin, and Christian Louboutin. In addition to the wide selection of Cuban cigars, there are colorful ceramic ashtrays, leather cigar cases, a sturdy desktop cigar cutter, elegantly textured metal lighters, and small humidors in which to properly store one's purchases at home. Peppered around the store are Winston Churchill collectibles, including a variety of hefty china pieces bearing his image, in honor of the iconic politician's first adult apartment, located next door at number 105. There is a second Sautter location in Knightsbridge at 8 Raphael Street.

106 MOUNT STREET . W1K 2TW ♣ GREEN PARK ☎ 020 7581 5898

🌐 SAUTTERCIGARS.COM

Penfriend

Nestled in Burlington Arcade's row of luxury boutiques is Penfriend—the British term for pen pal—which sells impeccably crafted, high-quality pens that make correspondence and journal writing a true pleasure. Although the shop carries new pieces by companies such as Montblanc, Visconti, and Caran d'Ache, the real draw for many clients is the well-chosen array of antique writing instruments, with an emphasis on midcentury fountain pens made by companies such as Waterman and Parker. Unlike what one might find in a flea market or in an elderly relative's attic, everything here is in pristine condition, from the colorful enamel exteriors to the precise gold nibs. Also on hand is an array of ballpoints, rollerballs, and mechanical pencils, both old and new. Expert pen repair and engraving are available in a workshop at Penfriend's second location at 17 Fleet Street.

34 BURLINGTON ARCADE . W1J 0QA 🚇 GREEN PARK ☎ 020 7499 6337
🌐 PENFRIEND.CO.UK

Sounds of the Universe

In the heart of Soho, inside a tile-lined building that once housed a pub and a rehearsal room favored by the Rolling Stones in their early days, this quintessential music fan's record shop is lined with packed bins of vinyl and, almost always, shoppers methodically rifling through them. The specialty is electronic music, but there's also a vast selection of reggae, alternative music, and rock classics on both of its two floors, along with hard-to-find music books. The staff is always happy to make suggestions of music that's new or old; they are extremely well versed in many musical genres, reflected by the music played in-store on a set of turntables.

7 BROADWICK ST . W1F 0DA 🏛 PICCADILLY CIRCUS ☎ 020 7734 3430

🌐 SOUNDSOFTHEUNIVERSE.COM

James Smith & Sons

Since 1830, this large store, which bills itself as the "home of the London umbrella," has specialized in manufacturing and selling beautifully crafted umbrellas, parasols, seat sticks, canes, and walking sticks for men and women. The store's original fittings are still intact, so stepping inside takes you back into another time, and a refined, genteel one at that. Though the majority of the items are investments, such as a men's umbrella topped with a curved handle in solid maple, or in oak with a sterling silver band, there are more moderately priced full-sized and folding umbrellas for men and women, including some with ornately carved handles in the shape of owls or the heads of long-billed ducks. The staff is approachable and friendly; an on-site workshop offers repair and refurbishment services.

53 NEW OXFORD STREET . WC1A 1BL 🚇 TOTTENHAM COURT ROAD/HOLBORN ☎ 020 7836 4731
🌐 JAMES-SMITH.CO.UK

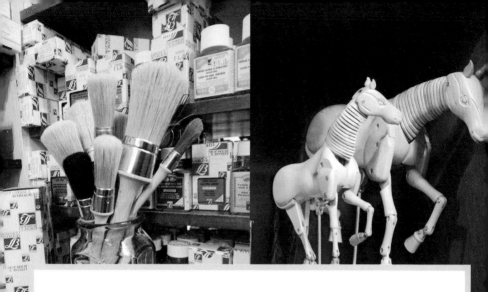

L. Cornelissen & Son

Since 1855, this accommodating Bloomsbury shop has been renowned for selling high-quality and hard-to-find artist's tools and materials, from fine sable brushes to a wide range of specialty papers, primed canvases, rare pigments, gouache, gilding materials, and much more. It's a place that London's most acclaimed visual artists rely on for their supplies—although the discreet staff won't ever divulge names—but amateurs are welcomed warmly as well. The shop has a loyal, globally based clientele and ships worldwide.

105 GREAT RUSSELL STREET . WC1B 3RY 🚇 HOLBORN ☎ 020 7636 1045

🌐 CORNELISSEN.COM

Grays of Westminster

Although it sells only one brand of camera—Nikon—this refined store has been attracting both amateur and professional photographers, including legends such as the late director Stanley Kubrick, for decades. In fact, it appeals to a loyal clientele from around the world. The shop's atmosphere is a major aspect of its appeal: outfitted with leather-topped wooden desks instead of counters, ornate molding on the ceiling, and an all-male staff in suits, Grays is at once old school and swanky, offering impeccable service and advice. Nonetheless, even new customers coming in for a small point-and-shoot digital pocket camera or a new memory card are treated like VIPs buying an elaborate piece of equipment. Downstairs, there's a huge archive of vintage and collectible Nikons, including both standard cameras and one-off rarities, making that area of the store not unlike a small museum, except that everything is for sale.

40 CHURTON STREET . SW1V 2LP ♛ PIMLICO/VICTORIA ☎ 020 7828 4925
🌐 GRAYSOFWESTMINSTER.CO.UK

Olive Loves Alfie

Olive Loves Alfie is filled with stylish spins on necessities for kids. Here you'll find baby onesies and long johns adorned with Bengal tigers or hot pink stars, toddler-sized Dr. Martens and tiny fringed moccasins, and snazzy bright yellow raincoats. There are also home items for kids' rooms such as handstitched cotton muslin bed quilts and melamine dishware; a range of birthday party gear, from bright decorations to paper cups and plates; and a selection of lovely, mostly wooden and gadget-free toys. There is a second location at 6 Victory Parade in the East Village.

84 STOKE NEWINGTON CHURCH STREET . N16 0AP 🚇 STOKE NEWINGTON
☎ 020 7241 4212 🌐 OLIVELOVESALFIE.CO.UK

Mungo & Maud

For Chelsea and Belgravia's affluent pet owners, this is *the* place for stylish dog and cat essentials. Located on Elizabeth Street—an appealing stretch of a few blocks near Eaton Square lined with upscale boutiques and little cafés—the store offers its own brand of collars in muted colors, beautifully knit wool toys, leashes, and feeding bowls that you'd actually want to display instead of hide in a corner of the kitchen. The dog beds—upholstered like expensive sofa cushions, covered in charcoal gray cotton or a gingham print in powder blue and white—are truly covetable. The prices are on the high side but worth it; the goods are of impeccable quality and have infinitely more panache than what's available in a typical neighborhood pet store.

79 ELIZABETH STREET . SW1W 9PJ 🚇 SLOANE SQUARE ☎ 020 7022 1207
🌐 MUNGOANDMAUD.COM

Rough Trade West

Rough Trade has been a nerve center of alternative music in London for more than forty years, continuing to thrive even with increased competition from downloads and online music sharing. Although this west London branch is modestly sized, it's crammed with vinyl records, from the commonly available to the obscure. The staff is music obsessed, so they're happy to talk and to make suggestions of both recent releases and underground gems.

130 TALBOT ROAD . W11 1JA 🚇 LADBROKE GROVE ☎ 020 7229 8541
🌐 ROUGHTRADE.COM

Rough Trade East

Rough Trade's other London outpost, located in a former beer factory in Shoreditch, is as much a place for music aficionados to gather as it is to pick up the latest album by a popular alternative band. There are, of course, loads of CDs and albums, but there's also an inviting café in the front; in the back, there's an area that hosts personal appearances, book signings, and intimate short concerts by critically acclaimed artists. There's even an old-school photo booth for taking instant black-and-white shots. Designed by renowned architect David Adjaye, the store is filled with fervent fans most evenings and all day on weekends—it's a constant swirl of activity that truly adds to the vibrant atmosphere.

OLD TRUMAN BREWERY, 91 BRICK LANE . E1 6QL 🚇 LIVERPOOL STREET; SHOREDITCH HIGH STREET
☎ 020 7392 7788 ⊕ ROUGHTRADE.COM

Rachel Vosper

In her appealing boutique, Rachel Vosper creates and sells beguilingly scented candles, hand poured in a tiny area in the back of the shop and packaged in colorful textured leather sleeves as well as the more usual glass. The fragrances tend toward the subtle and refined in both customary varieties, such as French lavender and jasmine, and less common ones, such as echinacea and Mexican orange blossom. Vosper and her team offer candle-making lessons monthly and create custom-scented candles for a growing number of local and international clients. Located just a few minutes from the bustling shopping hub that includes Harrods and Harvey Nichols, the shop feels as though it could be in a quiet village in the British countryside, as it's on a hidden little street that's also home to a minimalist women's clothing store (Egg), an excellent Pakistani restaurant (Salloos), and—as is so often the case in Britain—an atmospheric, popular pub, The Nag's End.

69 KINNERTON STREET . SW1X 8ED 🚇 HYDE PARK CORNER/KNIGHTSBRIDGE ☎ 020 7235 9666
🌐 RACHELVOSPER.COM

Davenports Magic Shop

Open since 1898 and still run by the same family that launched it, Davenports is London's definitive source of magic tricks: special card decks, disappearing balls and cups, coins that can appear to vanish and be found behind one's ear, and much more. It caters to both aspiring and professional magicians. Although it's across from Charing Cross station, the discreet location down a small set of stairs makes it more of a savvy secret than a busy West End boutique. The cordial, easygoing staff is well versed in all sorts of magic tricks and is happy to perform them as well as to make recommendations to practitioners of all levels and ages. Classes are available for kids and adults in the Magic Studio adjacent to the shop, while a makeshift museum next to the main sales area has a display of offbeat vintage magic-related collectibles, too, some of which belonged to the store's founder.

7 CHARING CROSS UNDERGROUND ARCADE, THE STRAND . WC2N 4HZ 🚇 CHARING CROSS
☎ 020 7836 0408 🌐 DAVENPORTSMAGIC.CO.UK

VV Rouleaux

Tucked off boutique-lined Marylebone High Street, a short stroll from Oxford Street, VV Rouleaux is an appealing shop with a distinct specialty: ribbons. Stretching over two floors, the store offers an immense selection, from colorful, thick bands of grosgrain to delicate lengths of slender silk in many shades and widths. You'll also find feathers and silk flowers to decorate hats and fascinators, the embellished toppers often worn by British women at weddings and events such as the Royal Ascot. Throughout the year, the store offers ribbon-related courses, from a single lesson in fashioning tassels and Turk's-head knots to an intensive workshop in making flowers.

102 MARYLEBONE LANE . W1U 2QD 🚇 BOND STREET ☎ 020 7224 5179
🌐 VVROULEAUX.COM

Marby & Elm

A letterpress design shop, Marby & Elm creates customized stationery and also sells a full line of gorgeous paper products hand-printed on a vintage letter press—cards, tags, journals, coasters, and notepads. You'll also find pencils in a range of neon colors, printed tote bags, paperweights, wooden pencil boxes, rubber stamps, and other sundries. In contrast to some of London's more traditional stationers, the vibe here, both of the paper goods and of the store itself, is a bit sassy and always fun, due in part to the fact that Marby & Elm is a family business: the founder is the daughter of a lettering artist, and her two siblings are part of the store's team.

33 CLERKENWELL ROAD . EC1M 5RN 🚇 FARRINGDON/BARBICAN ☎ 020 3609 9972

🌐 MARBYANDELM.COM

MARKETS

Although London's stores and boutiques are dynamic, there's really nothing more exhilarating than spending a few hours at a market that's crowded with passionate customers perusing an eclectic lineup of unique offerings—be they antiques, collectibles, clothing, or foodstuffs—juxtaposed in a way you'd never find in even the most diversely stocked department store or food hall. London has a unique array of flea and antiques markets, some of which are centrally located, selling everything from kitschy inexpensive knickknacks to valuable keepsakes. There are many food markets that feature inventive street bites worthy of a critically lauded restaurant, as well as high-quality produce and packaged goods that are delicious finds to bring home. The settings aren't necessarily polished or orderly—in fact, the cacophony is often part of the fun. But the city's best markets—both indoor setups of vendors and outdoor stalls that attract throngs of shoppers, even on blustery winter days—are not-to-miss, colorful destinations at which you can find antique treasures, quirky delicacies, or just a bargain, surrounded by locals attracted by precisely the same things.

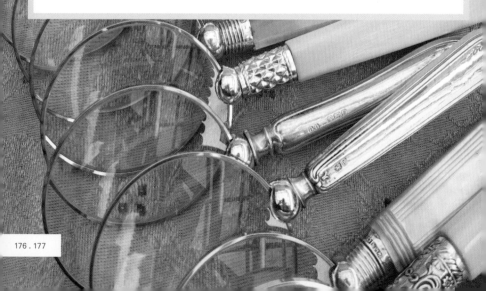

ALFIES ANTIQUE MARKET

This huge North London space, which brings together more than seventy-five dealers over five floors in a large art deco–style building, is an excellent resource for eighteenth-century teacups and dishes; precious antique jewelry, especially from the Victorian and art deco eras; World War II trench art; and midcentury furniture, among other treasures. Though it's a touch more refined than a typical outdoor flea market, you'll still find customers chatting and negotiating with dealers, many of whom are flexible on prices. It's a favorite of decorators as well as interior designers looking for inspiration, due to its diverse selection of attractive, high-quality items. Although the clientele is mostly Londoners, most vendors are happy to ship worldwide.

13–25 CHURCH STREET . NW8 8DT 🚇 MARYLEBONE ☎ 020 7723 6066 ⊕ ALFIESANTIQUES.COM

BOROUGH MARKET

Walking through this enormous covered food hall is an intoxicating, enchanting experience for the senses: there are bright displays of local and exotic produce, vendors touting freshly baked bread and smoky Spanish *salchichón*, the potent aroma of paella sizzling on a giant pan to be dished out in lunch-size portions, and—invariably—huge crowds of hungry food lovers. The selection of imported European delicacies, including pantry items such as tinned foie gras and unfiltered olive oil, is especially robust; truly impossible to resist are the crusty baguettes from Olivier's Bakery and Bianca e Mora's sublime Parmigiano Reggiano.

8 SOUTHWARK STREET . SE1 1TL 🚇 LONDON BRIDGE ☎ 020 7407 1002 ⊕ BOROUGHMARKET.ORG.UK

BRIXTON MARKET

This extremely lively market, which includes several covered arcades as well as expanses of sidewalks nearby, reflects the culinary and cultural preferences of Brixton's African and Caribbean communities, with several dozen vendors selling exotic ingredients and colorful imported textiles. The complex has also had an influx of new businesses over the last few years, including Federation Coffee, an always crowded spot for cappuccinos and pastries, and adorable gift boutiques such as Homestore, which stocks printed Finnish linens as well as patterned ceramic mugs and plates made nearby. Though there's a mix of different sensibilities—ethnic and cool-and-somewhat-gentrified—somehow they fit together seamlessly in animated, noisy harmony. There's always something to discover, buy, or eat at this market, making it popular among both Brixton residents and Londoners from all over the city.

ELECTRIC AVENUE . SW9 8LX 🚇 BRIXTON ☎ NO TELEPHONE ⊕ BRIXTONMARKET.NET

CAMDEN PASSAGE

Not to be confused with Camden Market—which gets very crowded, mostly with tourists—Camden Passage is a small street filled with independently owned boutiques. Many shops there specialize in specific antiques, from Hearts & Daggers' medals and military paraphernalia to Turn On Lighting's vast choice of lamps from 1850 to 1950. On most days, a cluster of outdoor vintage dealers sets up shop in a few alcoves along the row: the focus is on vintage jewelry, silverware, china, and bric-a-brac on Wednesday and Saturday mornings; all sorts of books—from hardcover collectibles to inexpensive paperbacks—are sold on Sundays, Thursdays, and Fridays.

CAMDEN PASSAGE . N1 8EA 🚇 ANGEL ☎ NO TELEPHONE ⊕ CAMDENPASSAGEISLINGTON.CO.UK

COLUMBIA ROAD FLOWER MARKET

Every Sunday morning, regardless of the weather, Londoners from all over the city head to this superb flower market. The quality here is remarkable: fresh tulips just flown in from Amsterdam, locally grown lavender with its distinctive aroma wafting down the street, deep red roses with their tight petals poised to bloom perfectly a couple of days after purchase. The market opens at 8:00 A.M. and is extremely crowded by about 9:00, even on mornings that are cold or damp, but it is a true Londoners' experience that's an absolute treat for the senses.

COLUMBIA ROAD . E2 7RG 🚇 OLD STREET/BETHNAL GREEN ☎ NO TELEPHONE
⊕ COLUMBIAROAD.INFO

GRAYS ANTIQUE CENTRE

Grays is an assembly of about two hundred antique dealers spread out over two cavernous floors in two buildings off South Molton Street, right near Oxford and Bond streets; it's where true antique connoisseurs come to find keepsakes. What's on sale is diverse, collectible, and of high quality, from Chinese Chongzhen vases to Edwardian dolls with fluttering eyelashes, from delicate Victorian engagement rings to art deco watches. Although most of Grays' dealers are open on Saturday, not all are, so it's best to come on a weekday and to allow plenty of time to canvass the large space.

58 DAVIES STREET AND 1–7 DAVIES MEWS . W1K 5AB 🚇 BOND STREET ☎ 020 7629 7034
⊕ GRAYSANTIQUES.COM

HAMMERSMITH VINTAGE FASHION FAIR

Held on select Sundays throughout the year in a large municipal building in Hammersmith, this fair draws in fashion magazine editors and designers among the many regulars who come to hunt for used and vintage clothing spanning many eras through the 1970s. Among the covetable finds: embroidered handkerchiefs, an array of buttons from the 1920s, weathered World War II–era military jackets, structured crocodile handbags from the 1950s, and collectible Ossie Clark dresses.

HAMMERSMITH TOWN HALL, KING STREET . W6 9JU 🚇 HAMMERSMITH/RAVENSCOURT PARK
☎ NO TELEPHONE ⊕ PA-ANTIQUES.CO.UK/LONDONVINTAGEFASHIONFAIR.HTML

MALTBY STREET MARKET

Borough Market may be bigger and better known, but Maltby Street Market, a weekend gathering of a couple dozen food stalls in South London, has become where the city's most ardent foodies come for just-baked loafs of tangy sourdough bread and flaky salted caramel brownies as well as quirky street food, such as Scotch eggs prepared with spicy, paprika-laden chorizo by Finest Fayre and Waffle On's buttermilk-batter waffles topped with Chinese-style roast duck and plum sauce. Be sure to try Hansen & Lydersen's thickly cut, dill-topped cold-smoked salmon, too. Arriving early is advisable, as this is a small market on a narrow, centuries-old street; typically it's quite crowded by around 11 A.M.

LASSCO ROPEWALK, 41 MALTBY STREET . SE1 3PA 🚇 BERMONDSEY ☎ NO TELEPHONE
⊕ MALTBY.ST

MARYLEBONE FARMERS' MARKET

On Sunday mornings, a large parking lot off Marylebone High Street fills up with vendors selling goat's-milk cheese from Sussex, apples from Kent, freshly baked, crusty baguettes, and shucked Norfolk oysters to eat on the premises. Open in the winter and even if it's raining, this is an easy-to-navigate set of outdoor stalls with uniformly high-quality foods sold at a central location that makes it an easy, quick stop for delectable provisions for many Londoners.

CRAMER STREET CAR PARK, CRAMER STREET . W1U 4EW 🚇 BOND STREET/MARBLE ARCH
☎ NO TELEPHONE ⊕ LFM.ORG.UK/MARKETS/MARYLEBONE

OLD SPITALFIELDS MARKET

Old Spitalfields Market has been a hub for street vendors since 1887; over the last couple of decades, as the neighborhood has been developed and gentrified, it has become more popular than ever. Under its open-air roof are tables at which sellers offer a wide range of items—vintage biker jackets, scarves from Nepal, vintage eyeglasses, silk-screened T-shirts, and trendy leather handbags—with permanent stores around the market edges too. (Inspitalfields, for example, is an excellent source of quirky home items and gifts.) Food has a heavy presence, too, including Flying Angels of Spitalfields, which sells indulgent baked goods such as baklava and brownies, and branches of London chains including Leon and The Real Greek.

109 COMMERCIAL STREET . E1 6BG 🚇 LIVERPOOL STREET; SHOREDITCH HIGH STREET
☎ 020 7247 8556 ⊕ OLDSPITALFIELDSMARKET.COM

PIMLICO CAR BOOT SALE

Car boot sales—at which people sell their unwanted old things, customarily out of their cars' trunks—are an institution in the United Kingdom. At Pimlico's well-organized version, held on Sundays year-round, it's often possible to find an incredibly cheap designer item or piece of collectible china among the sea of bric-a-brac here. The best spots in which to hunt for treasures are indoors, on tables set up inside what during the week is a large room within a school.

PIMLICO ACADEMY, CHICESTER STREET ENTRANCE, LUPUS STREET . SW1V 3AT
🚇 PIMLICO OR VICTORIA ☎ NO TELEPHONE ⊕ CAPITALCARBOOT.COM

PORTOBELLO MARKET

Portobello Road hosts one of London's best-known markets, a sprawl of more than one thousand vendors. The market gets extremely crowded, especially on Saturdays. Although there are, especially near the Notting Hill Gate end, souvenir T-shirts and cheap scarves on offer, it's still a wonderful source of antiques if you know where to go. There is, for example, a cluster of nearly two hundred dealers inside the Admiral Vernon Antique Market at number 141–149, where you can find Victorian china, collectible jewelry, antique memorabilia relating to the royal family, and oil paintings that are mostly more ornamental than highly valuable but still worth bringing home. There are also a few not-to-miss culinary treats on Portobello Road, including authentic Spanish groceries at R. Garcia and Sons at 248–250 and Portuguese *pastel de nata* tarts at Lisboa Patisserie at 57 Golborne Road nearby.

PORTOBELLO ROAD . W11 1LA 🚇 NOTTING HILL GATE/LADBROKE GROVE ☎ NO TELEPHONE
⊕ PORTOBELLOROAD.CO.UK

FOOD AND DRINK

London's food scene is creative, expressive, international, and filled with a myriad of options, whether you're looking for a freshly baked croissant and foam-topped latte or a gourmand-worthy dinner to celebrate a special occasion. While London has spawned acclaimed, world-renowned chefs, including Gordon Ramsay and Jamie Oliver— both of whom still have their hands in several of the city's restaurants—some of its most appealing culinary experiences have a quieter charm. If you know where to go, there are many options for delicious food served without too much fanfare or drama in informal, welcoming spaces nestled within the city's residential neighborhoods. Likewise, though many of London's esteemed restaurants are expensive, there are plenty of fantastic spots beloved by local foodies, in addition to quintessentially dark, atmospheric pubs and fish and chip shops that are considerably more affordable. One experience that tends to be enjoyed more by visitors than locals, but is still not to miss, is afternoon tea, a splurge well worth the indulgence.

RESTAURANTS

As London is a truly international, cosmopolitan city, it's not all that surprising that many of its most enticing restaurants specialize in cuisines that are anything but English. Many focus on authentic recipes from other countries, prepared with top-notch ingredients, whether what's served is squid ink linguine, *saag paneer*, *shakshuka*, *siu mai*, or sushi. Of equally delicious note are the city's more inventive restaurants that put their own unique twists on ethnic cooking. And, of course, there are still wonderful spots to get British classics cooked to perfection, including hard-to-beat indulgences such as sticky toffee pudding that are worth every extravagant calorie.

Bocca di Lupo

This enticing restaurant serves authentic dishes originating throughout Italy rather than the cuisine of a single region, and the food—from Piedmontese *agnolotti dal plin* to Sicilian grilled prawns with garlicky *gremolata*—is always authentic and delicious. Although it's in Soho, Bocca di Lupo is easy to miss—it's located down a short street that runs behind the Apollo Theater—but has loyal devotees, so reservations are a must. The dishes are designed to be shared; superlative options include pasta smothered with luscious duck ragù, tomato-sauced risotto flecked with succulent Italian prawns, cold-weather-appropriate creamy polenta, and golden fried *bocconcini*. If there's room for dessert, the espresso gelato—made at Gelupo, the restaurant's ice cream shop across the street—is a popular choice.

12 ARCHER STREET . W1D 7BB 🚇 PICCADILLY CIRCUS ☎ 020 7734 2223
🌐 BOCCADILUPO.COM

Rochelle Canteen

The name of this always packed restaurant isn't for effect—it's actually on the grounds of a school, in a small low-frills building that was once used for bicycle storage, its entrance behind a door with a poorly marked bell. A few minutes' walk from Shoreditch High Street, the food and the character of the place make it worth searching out. The menu, which changes daily, includes spins on British comfort food, such as savory veal meatballs with buttery mashed potatoes as well as sticky toffee pudding. There is also a simple but well-prepared breakfast menu that includes house-made granola with poached seasonal fruit and toast made from freshly baked bread, served with chunky jam or Britain's beloved Marmite.

ROCHELLE SCHOOL, ARNOLD CIRCUS . E2 7ES 🚇 SHOREDITCH HIGH STREET ☎ 020 7729 5677

🌐 ARNOLDANDHENDERSON.COM/4-ROCHELLE_CANTEEN.HTML

The Palomar

Just a few blocks from London's Chinatown, this critically lauded restaurant serves cutting-edge Israeli food, blending influences from continental Europe, Africa, and the Middle East into a menu that includes *bourekas* and challah bread. The *fattoush* salad, with large shards of crusty bread and house-made tangy *labneh*, is sublime; thinly sliced beets daubed with an irrepressibly sweet blend of dates and honey are complex and comforting; and the extra-tender pork belly tagine is the perfect balance of sweet and spicy. Although the dining room, located in the back of the restaurant, is a refined spot for a meal, the best seats are at the bar up front, where watching the chefs work their magic is part of the experience.

34 RUPERT STREET . W1D 6DN 🚇 PICCADILLY CIRCUS ☎ 020 7439 8777
🌐 THEPALOMAR.CO.UK

A. Wong

Many people wouldn't expect to find stellar Chinese food in London; similarly, most Londoners would doubt the excellence of a restaurant located a couple of blocks from the major transportation hub that is Victoria Station. Dismiss your preconceptions: the food here really is fabulous, overseen by Andrew Wong, who took over his father's more predictable restaurant and turned it into a creative, upscale amalgamation of dishes from all over China. Lunch, when dim sum is served, is the star meal; one highlight: a splendidly earthy, tiny steamed bun with truffle and wild mushroom, glazed to resemble its filling and served on a bed of grass. In the evenings, there are plates of glossy-skinned Peking duck and an inventive ten-course menu.

70 WILTON ROAD . SW1V 1DE 🚇 VICTORIA ☎ 020 7828 8931
🌐 AWONG.CO.UK

The Modern Pantry

This airy Clerkenwell restaurant is distinguished by its inventive, ethnically inspired takes on classic European dishes, such as soft omelettes packed with meaty, sugar-cured prawns and topped with a healthy dollop of house-made sambal and tender grilled steak marinated in miso and tamarind. Nonetheless, it's a casual neighborhood place to which locals come for a quick breakfast or to sit outside on a sunny day with a cappuccino in hand. The best drink is, arguably, the hot chocolate, available in three varieties, including an intensely flavorful option infused with licorice and Urfa chili. Also served is an original afternoon tea, with flaky scones made with sun-dried tomatoes, Parmesan, and mustard seed or with rose water and sour cherries. There is a second location at 14 Finsbury Square.

47–48 ST. JOHN'S SQUARE . EC1V 4JJ 🚇 FARRINGDON ☎ 020 7553 9210
🌐 THEMODERNPANTRY.CO.UK

Honey & Co.

When strolling down Warren Street—an unpretentious stretch of modest, independently run businesses—it would be easy to overlook this laid-back spot. But don't: the profoundly flavorsome food at Honey & Co. is just too good to miss. The Israeli husband-and-wife team Sarit Packer and Itamar Srulovich—both veterans of London's acclaimed restaurant Ottolenghi—serve perfectly executed takes on Middle Eastern classics such as hummus, tender lamb shawarma, and greaseless falafel in a compact, sparsely decorated space that's all about the food. Breakfast here is also a highlight, thanks to offerings such as *shakshuka*, or eggs baked in either a savory tomato sauce or complexly spiced spinach, and creamy yogurt topped with deeply sweet roasted plums and house-made puffed wheat cereal.

25A WARREN STREET . W1T 5LZ 🚇 GREAT PORTLAND STREET/WARREN STREET ☎ 020 7388 6175
🌐 HONEYANDCO.CO.UK

Sushi Tetsu

A seat at this über-authentic Japanese sushi bar, wedged into a tiny lane in Clerkenwell, is one of London's hardest-to-get restaurant reservations—and it's easy to understand why. It is extremely small—just seven seats—and serves some of the freshest, best-cut, most exquisitely marinated fish imaginable. There's also a theatrical flair to the way chef Toru Takahashi prepares everything in front of his diners' eyes: swiping unctuous concentrated soy sauce across slabs of eel with a thick brush; searing vinegar-marinated mackerel with a lit blowtorch; grating brightly flavored fresh yuzu rind onto tender whitefish. Omakase—a multicourse meal consisting of dishes chosen by the chef—is the way to go, although ordering à la carte is also an option.

12 JERUSALEM PASSAGE . EC1V 4JP 🚇 FARRINGDON/BARBICAN ☎ 020 3217 0090
🌐 SUSHITETSU.CO.UK

Tayyabs

There are many excellent Indian restaurants in London, but many locals consider this to be the city's best, well worth the trek to Whitechapel in London's East End. The quality of the ingredients is outstanding, and a key part of what's so special here in dishes such as large prawns enrobed in spices and quickly roasted in the tandoori oven, bright and fresh vegetables such as pumpkin, and spinach and okra in complexly flavored curries. The upbeat atmosphere is also highly appealing and makes it an ideal place for a celebration. The food is so good that regular patrons come specifically for special dishes that are available only once a week, such as *haleem*, a comforting, intensely flavored stew of extra-tender lamb and lentils, that's served just on Sundays.

83–89 FIELDGATE STREET . E1 1JU 🚇 ALDGATE EAST ☎ 020 7247 9543
🌐 TAYYABS.CO.UK

Lemonia

This friendly, pretty restaurant that serves consistently delicious Greek food is a perennial favorite on Regent's Park Road, the charming main drag of Primrose Hill, a leafy, residential neighborhood just north of central London. Standouts here include the *spanakopita*—verdant green spinach and just-sharp-enough feta cheese swaddled in crunchy layers of phyllo pastry—and grilled skewers of succulent lamb, chicken, or pork. Lemonia attracts a wide range of locals: families in the early evening, couples out for a quiet dinner, and, quite frequently, one of the celebrities who live nearby. It gets busy at lunch as well as at dinner, so booking ahead is recommended, as is coming in the summertime, when the outdoor seating in front affords a perfect view of the passing parade.

89 REGENT'S PARK ROAD . NW1 8UY 🚇 CHALK FARM ☎ 020 7586 7454
🌐 LEMONIA.CO.UK

La Cuisine de Bar by Poilâne

Poilâne bread—malty, dense, thick crusted, and as delicious plain as slathered with butter or jam—is virtually synonymous with Paris, but its beloved bakery has two London outposts: a take-out storefront on Elizabeth Street and this charming café nestled just off Sloane Square that's humming with neighborhood devotees all day long, from chic moms in the morning to executives coming in for a glass of Chablis and light bite at the end of the day. The stars of the menu are the tartines: slabs of delectable bread topped with everything from smooth foie gras to honey to gooey Saint-Marcellin cheese and cured ham.

39 CADOGAN GARDENS . SW3 2TB 🚇 SLOANE SQUARE ☎ 020 3263 6019
🌐 CUISINEDEBAR.FR

Peckham Bazaar

This compact, unfussy restaurant describes itself as Pan-Balkan, a roundabout way of explaining the multicultural twists of some of the unusual and unusually delicious dishes it serves up: grilled chicken revved up with earthy Egyptian *dukkah* and creamy, garlicky Greek *skordalia*, oniony Turkish *imam bayildi* with creamy *labneh*, marinated octopus spiked with capers and served over a tangy bed of white tarama. The combinations feel natural, not contrived, making it popular among the neighborhood's young, creative types and fervent foodies who frequent it regularly.

119 CONSORT ROAD . SE15 3RU 🚇 PECKHAM RYE ☎ 020 7732 2525
🌐 PECKHAMBAZAAR.COM

Clarke's

There's a whiff of California in some of the dishes at this top-notch Notting Hill mainstay, with its focus on seasonal ingredients and dishes such as a fruit-laden, brioche-crusted tart inspired by the acclaimed Los Angeles–based baker Nancy Silverton. But Sally Clarke's delectable cooking is rooted in Great Britain and is distinctly European, as are many of her best-in-class ingredients, including brill from Cornwall enlivened with flavorful salsa verde or the saline touches of black olive tapenade, crisp-skinned duck from Lancashire, and Scottish salmon that's served with free-range eggs in the morning and with crème fraîche later in the day. Across the street, Clarke runs a bakery and gourmet grocery that is well stocked with mouthwatering baked goods, prepared foods, and excellent pantry items including house-made fruit jams and chunky, bright marmalade.

124 KENSINGTON CHURCH STREET . W8 4BH 🚇 NOTTING HILL GATE ☎ 020 7221 9225
🌐 SALLYCLARKE.COM/RESTAURANT

Bonnie Gull Seafood Shack

A loyal, regular crowd frequents this unpretentious neighborhood spot that serves extremely fresh and flavorful fish, all sourced from Great Britain. The shellfish, like cockles from Dorset and West Sussex crab, is exceptionally good, whether served as individual dishes, or as part of an assorted platter or a richly flavored bouillabaisse. But really, everything on the menu is delicious, including the potatoes fried indulgently in beef drippings. British beers are also served, including Scottish Schiehallion Craft Lager, an ingredient in Bonnie Gull's caramel-hued batter for fish and chips.

21A FOLEY STREET . W1W 6DS 🚇 GREAT PORTLAND STREET/OXFORD CIRCUS ☎ 020 7436 0921
🌐 BONNIEGULLSEAFOODSHACK.COM

Berber & Q

This critically acclaimed casual restaurant in Haggerston—in East London, not all that far from Shoreditch and Dalston—is the sort of place you'd come with a group of your coolest friends for a festive evening with loud music, cleverly conceived cocktails, and, most notably, delicious Middle Eastern–inspired food. The main attraction is the assortment of grilled meat—cumin-smeared lamb, sumac-laden sausages, chicken thighs rubbed in apricot and nutty *dukkah*. The lamb and beef are sourced from a family-run purveyor in north Wales. For noncarnivores, a wide selection of mostly vegetarian mezze is available as well; smoky eggplant and cauliflower shawarma are standouts. Perennially crowded, Berber & Q doesn't accept reservations, so it's best to come early or be prepared for a lengthy wait for a table.

ARCH 338, ACTON MEWS . E8 4EA 🚇 HAGGERSTON ☎ 020 7923 0829
🌐 BERBERANDQ.COM

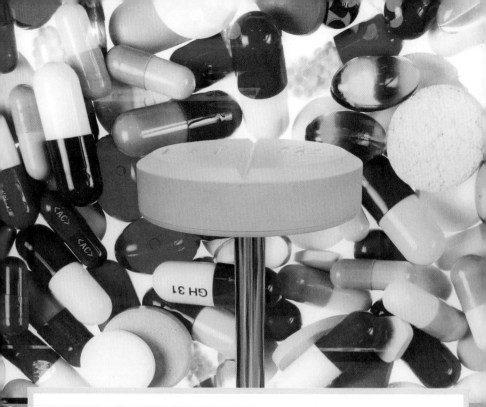

Pharmacy 2

Located above the artist Damien Hirst's Newport Street Gallery (page 26), this colorful restaurant—an updated take on a similar spot he conceived in the early 1990s—feels somewhat like walking into one of his pop culture–inspired works. Images of pills abound—on the back of chairs and banquettes, in a mural behind the bar, splashed across the walls—creating an edgy yet whimsical environment. Hirst partnered with the acclaimed restaurateur Mark Hix for a delicious menu that features top-quality local ingredients and has a slant toward comfort food, including linguine mixed with Dorset crab and shards of crimson chili and saffron-hued Bruford brown eggs soft-scrambled with De Beauvoir smoked salmon. Although the well-curated art exhibitions that are on display in the ground-floor gallery are always worth a look, the food and decor make Pharmacy 2 a popular destination unto itself, with many patrons coming simply for a tasty meal in a vibrant setting.

NEWPORT STREET . SE11 6AJ 🚇 KENSINGTON/VAUXHALL/LAMBETH NORTH/WATERLOO
☎ 020 3141 9333 ⊕ PHARMACYRESTAURANT.COM

Bob Bob Ricard

Sitting on one of Bob Bob Ricard's art deco–inspired, marine blue leather banquettes, it's impossible not to feel at least a little bit glamorous. This glitzy Soho spot serves up an array of indulgences—lobster macaroni and cheese, beef Wellington, caviar, salmon tartare, and oysters—alongside beautifully cooked Russian dishes such as shellfish *pelmeni* and butter-stuffed chicken Kiev. In keeping with the restaurant's sophisticated feel is a button at the side of each table that reads "Press for Champagne"; not surprisingly, the establishment proudly claims to pour more bubbly than any other restaurant in Great Britain.

1 UPPER JAMES STREET . W1F 9DF 🚇 PICCADILLY CIRCUS/OXFORD CIRCUS ☎ 020 3145 1000

🌐 BOBBOBRICARD.COM

Oldroyd

Tom Oldroyd, the chef and namesake of this likable Islington restaurant, is the former head chef of Polpo, a small chain of chic Italian eateries that serves creative but never fussy dishes with clean, bold flavors. There's a similar feel to the food, served in a warm atmosphere that makes even a visitor stopping by for the first time feel like a regular. Especially delicious is the spinach and ricotta malfatti—dumplings that are herbaceous and delicately prepared—as well as lightly fried croquettes filled with hearty mushrooms, English peas, or smoked haddock. The prices are extremely fair for food of this high caliber, especially at lunchtime, when a set menu is offered.

344 UPPER STREET . N1 0PD 🚇 ANGEL ☎ 020 8617 9010
🌐 OLDROYDLONDON.COM

The Book Club

It's certainly a restaurant—serving pesto-topped scrambled eggs in the morning and sustainably sourced grilled sea bass at lunch—but this relaxed space is essentially a split-level recreation room for East London's many cool kids. The sensibility is inclusive instead of intimidatingly hip, and there are events here all the time, from DJ nights to lectures, from craft workshops to literary salons. In the evening the bar menu of comfort food (burgers, nachos, and fajitas) accompanies a long list of beers, wine, and potent cocktails.

100–106 LEONARD STREET . EC2A 4RH 🚇 OLD STREET/LIVERPOOL STREET;
SHOREDITCH HIGH STREET ☎ 020 7684 8618 🌐 WEARETBC.COM

Black Axe Mangal

All over London, it's easy to find inexpensive takeout-focused spots specializing in *mangal*, a Turkish-style grilled meat, often served on fluffy pita-esque bread to eat as a wrap sandwich. But chef Lee Tierman's tiny *mangal* café in north London is truly unique: an unpretentious but gourmet-skewed kebab house with heavy metal music blaring in the background, images of the members of the rock band Kiss painted on the wood-burning oven, and a clientele of passionate foodies, neighbors, and cool kids out for the evening. A veteran of the gourmet meccas Noma and St. John, Tierman offers a creative and delicious menu, including options such as heavily spiced lamb offal, pork jowl, or mutton on top of transcendent, chewy, aerated bread. For accompaniment, there are spectacular cocktails by the award-winning mixologist Ryan Chetiyawardana, also known as Mr. Lyan.

156 CANONBURY ROAD . N1 2UP 🚇 HIGHBURY & ISLINGTON ☎ NO TELEPHONE
🌐 BLACKAXEMANGAL.COM

PUBS, GASTROPUBS, AND COCKTAIL BARS

The pub—the simple neighborhood spot in which to have a drink, get together with friends, and relax—is one of Britain's best-loved traditions. As the country's food scene has evolved over the last couple of decades, pubs have also become a place to find truly exceptional food, sometimes leaning toward hearty stalwarts—such as roast beef and burgers with chips—and often focusing on top-tier ingredients that are sourced locally. For something a bit more posh, London has elegant spots for a cocktail or glass of champagne as well as trendy bars that are ideal for people watching.

The Richmond

The Richmond is the sort of crisply designed, efficient, professional restaurant that feels as though it should be located in an upmarket residential community, yet it's a gem on a quiet corner in Dalston. A favorite among those who live nearby, it's also worth a trip, if only to sample its just-caught meaty oysters and wash them down with a shrunken Bloody Mary shooter. The seafood is terrific across the board, especially the fish stew with the hit of 'nduja sausage and sides such as Indian spiced spinach and crunchy French fries. The Richmond's founder, Brett Redman, also owns a lauded yakitori spot, Jidori, at 89 Kingsland High Street nearby.

316 QUEENSBRIDGE ROAD . E8 3NH 🚇 DALSTON KINGSLAND ☎ 010 7241 1638

🌐 THERICHMONDHACKNEY.COM

The Duck and Rice

This stylized pub on bustling Berwick Street, with daytime market stalls selling bargain-priced fruit outside, is the unlikely setting for first-class Chinese food made with top-quality ingredients. The creation of restaurateur Alan Yau, who also owns popular spots like Hakkasan and Yauatcha, has two floors. The downstairs menu offers mostly crunchy snacks such as salt-and-pepper squid and sesame prawn toast, accompanied by a long list of beers from all over the world, including fruity options from Belgium's Brouwerij van Honsebrouck that are an excellent counterfoil to the food. Upstairs, there's a more formal menu that's ideal for sharing; on weekends, a dim sum menu is served during the day. Not to miss are the transparent-skinned, shrimp-stuffed steamed har gau and shumai made with sweet, locally caught scallops.

90 BERWICK STREET . W1F 0QB 🚇 OXFORD CIRCUS/PICCADILLY CIRCUS ☎ 020 3327 7888
🌐 THEDUCKANDRICE.COM

The Champagne Room at The Connaught

The Connaught, nestled just off swanky Mount Street, is one of London's most luxurious hotels; in addition to the property's easily accessed dining locations, including a bright conservatory where afternoon tea is served, there is the somewhat hidden and rather glamorous Champagne Room, where you might imagine a 1930s film star coming for a clandestine date. Many guests— Londoners, too—don't even know it exists, but it's well worth venturing down a slender hallway adjacent to the lobby and heading to the right of the Connaught Bar. Once inside, you'll find champagne and well-mixed cocktails served in delicate Baccarat crystal glasses, surrounded by art deco furniture in a muted, elegant palette. The Champagne Bar doesn't accept reservations and can seat only about twenty-five guests, but since it's not a well-known spot, it's usually easy to find a seat.

CARLOS PLACE . W1K 2AL 🚇 GREEN PARK ☎ 020 7314 3419
🌐 THE-CONNAUGHT.CO.UK/MAYFAIR-BARS/CHAMPAGNE-ROOM

OUR BUTCHER
PHILIP WARRENS
NEWMAN ARMS
CORNWALL PROJECT
PORK SCRATCHINGS
£3 FROM THE BAR

Newman Arms

This atmospheric pub dates back to 1730, but the food menu reflects its focus on inventive modern cooking with top-quality ingredients, with dishes such as red mullet daubed with soy vinaigrette and roast lamb brightened with seaweed sauce. Thanks to a partnership with the Cornwall Project, an initiative that works with top Cornish farmers, fisherman, and butchers, everything on the menu is extra fresh, and what's on offer changes daily and with the season. Some of the pub's best beers are sourced from Cornwall, too, including Harbour Brewing Company's smooth ale and Cornish Orchards' still cider on tap, a notable draw to the after-work crowd that comes here to relax in the early evening on weeknights.

22 RATHBONE STREET . W1T 1NG 🚇 OXFORD CIRCUS/TOTTENHAM COURT ROAD ☎ 020 3643 6285
🌐 NEWMANARMSPUB.COM

69 Colebrooke Row

Located on a quiet corner in Islington, 69 Colebrooke Row derives its official name from its street address, but regulars know it as "The Bar with No Name," since this speakeasy-esque spot originally had no signage in front when it opened in 2009. It was one of the first of a new generation of cocktail bars with an old-school swagger, and its well-trained bartenders serve expertly blended drinks from behind a sleek wooden-topped bar, while red leather banquettes accentuate the space's 1950s feel. The drinks list changes seasonally and is anything but staid, although it is always possible to order standard cocktails such as a precisely mixed martini or Bloody Mary. To go with the beverages, such as the crisp and refreshing Death in Venice—a combination of Campari, Prosecco, and grapefruit bitters that brings to mind the Amalfi Coast more than the Angel Tube station—there are a few light bar snacks, including crunchy, twisted taralli biscuits imported from Italy.

69 COLEBROOKE ROW . N1 8AA 🚇 ANGEL ☎ 07540 528 593

🌐 69COLEBROOKEROW.COM

The Elgin

Though there are several pubs in London that bear the name Elgin, this one, in a residential neighborhood near Lord's Cricket Grounds and Abbey Road Studios, serves basic but finely prepared food in a very casual setting. On the ever-changing menu are excellent versions of standards—such as juicy cheeseburgers—and surprises, including a well-spiced vegetarian tagine and hot smoked trout with sea purslane. On weekend mornings, there's a leisurely feel, with couples lingering over newspapers and families dining with their young kids. Patronized mostly by people who live nearby, and offering a long list of affordable wines available by the glass and nine British beers on tap, the Elgin is a great spot for a chilled-out drink or meal.

255 ELGIN AVENUE . W9 1NJ 🚇 MAIDA VALE ☎ 020 7625 5511
🌐 THEELGIN.COM

Cahoots

The decor of this infectiously upbeat bar is intended to recall the use of the London Underground as an air-raid and bomb shelter during World War II, most notably during the Blitz from September 1940 through May 1941. To that end, some of the seating resembles a vintage train, and the cheerful waiters and waitresses dress in clothing from the period. Surprisingly, the concept doesn't come across as hokey; it works, helped along with bar snacks based on decidedly nongourmet delicacies from the era, such as Spam-and-cheese sandwiches, that are, yes, tasty. The cocktails, also in sync with the theme, are inventive, using ingredients that were prevalent in the era, such as the herbs and vegetables many British citizens grew during World War II food rationing. Centrally located at the heart of Carnaby Street, Cahoots is popular with everyone from twentysomethings to those who grew up hearing about wartime from parents who experienced it firsthand, so reservations are essential, even on weeknights.

13 KINGLY STREET . W1B 5PG 🚇 OXFORD CIRCUS ☎ 020 7352 6200
🌐 CAHOOTS-LONDON.COM

Marksman

Although East London has become one of London's trendiest neighborhoods, Marksman, on a corner near the spot where Columbia Road Flower Market (page 178) is held on Sunday, is a classic British pub at its best. That vibe is most pronounced on the main floor, which gets crowded, particularly on weekends, with an egalitarian blend of longtime community residents and a young, cool crowd that lives nearby. The tile-fronted building has housed a pub since the Victorian era; in the present incarnation, the food is as much a focus as the beverages, since the co-owners, Tom Harris and Jon Rotheram, are chefs who have worked with culinary notables such as Fergus Henderson and Jamie Oliver. The menu changes daily, with regular favorites such as plump mussels marinated in chili-infused vinaigrette served atop toasted, house-baked sourdough bread and flavorful roast duck on a bed of butternut square puree. A weekly highlight is the pub's Sunday lunch, at which high-quality, locally raised meat, including Hereford beef and chicken from Norfolk, is perfectly roasted and served with traditional English accompaniments such as Yorkshire pudding and bread sauce.

254 HACKNEY ROAD . E2 7SJ 🚇 HOXTON/SHOREDITCH HIGH STREET
☎ 020 7739 7393 🌐 MARKSMANPUBLICHOUSE.COM

The Last Tuesday Society

Although it serves tasty cocktails such as a white negroni with gin, vermouth, and herbal liqueur, the main attraction at this wonderfully dark East London bar is the decor. It's located inside the Viktor Wynd Museum of Curiosities, Fine Art & Natural History, a large collection of taxidermy, animal skeletons, and eccentric paraphernalia gathered by a local artist. Stuffed animals and artifacts abound; on the lower level, the displays include the bones of a lion, assembled as they would be in a natural history museum, with what's arguably the best table in the house situated right nearby. Some of the drinks served are in sync with the surroundings, such as the Scorpse Reviver, a take on a classic 1930s cocktail with absinthe and gin topped off with an edible dried scorpion.

11 MARE STREET . E8 4RP 🚇 CAMBRIDGE HEATH ☎ 020 7998 3617
🌐 THELASTTUESDAYSOCIETY.ORG

Baba

The vastly multicultural south London community of Peckham has been getting progressively more gentrified over the last few years, with a handful of spots that have become beloved among foodies as well as the new young residents and other Londoners who come by on weekends. Baba has been one of the community's focal points since its first incarnation, Ali Baba Juice, which whipped up highly unusual smoothies with puna yam and sumac in an outdoor space down an alley. Now located next door to another community favorite, Peckham Refreshment Rooms, Baba serves equally inventive drinks, both alcoholic and "virgin," plus intensely flavorful food that nods respectfully to the ethnic diversity of the neighborhood. Standouts include a sweet float with Guarana Antica soda, ice cream, and a lit sparkler popped inside the glass for dramatic decoration and, for accompaniment, *iman bayaldi*, a Turkish dish made with smoky eggplant, cinnamon, and raisins.

12–16 BLENHEIM GROVE, UNIT 5 . SW15 4QL 🚇 PECKHAM RYE ☎ NO TELEPHONE
🌐 BABAWORLD.CO.UK

The Thomas Cubitt

Located on charming Elizabeth Street and named for an acclaimed nineteenth-century architect who worked on part of Buckingham Palace, this friendly gastropub is on the upscale side, and its two floors are welcoming to all. The main floor, with its working fireplace and dark wood paneling, leans toward the more convivial and casual, serving lemongrass-infused gin and tonics as well as juicy burgers cooked rare and served with creamy bacon mayonnaise. There the feel is that of a classic pub, albeit one in a swank setting. Upstairs, both the atmosphere and the menu—including melt-in-your-mouth chicken poached in butter and accompanied by tangy balsamic-glazed shallots—are a bit more formal. Regulars make sure to save room for dessert, such as the warm chocolate tart with a generously sized dollop of clotted cream that's served on both floors.

44 ELIZABETH STREET . SW1W 9PA 🚇 SLOANE SQUARE ☎ 020 7730 6060

🌐 THETHOMASCUBITT.CO.UK

Redchurch Brewery

One way to find this unassuming Bethnal Green bar is to follow your nose: it's perched above a working brewery redolent with the pungent scents of hops and yeast. Upstairs sits the Tap Room, an intentionally low-frills but comfortable space that sells the brewery's craft beers, including dense, chocolatey, dark brown Hoxton Stout and delicate, smooth Great Eastern India Pale Ale. There is always a large handful of freshly made beers available on tap, but bottled options are sold here as well to either drink on the premises or take home. The crowd is mostly local and young; up-and-coming DJs and performances by emerging alternative bands act as the soundtrack most evenings. Though the Tap Room serves its just-brewed beer only a few evenings a week, it's a good choice as a final stop on a long evening out in the East End, as it stays open late and keeps buzzing with sometimes loud groups of local twentysomethings later than many drinking spots in London.

275–276 POYSER STREET . E2 9RF 🚇 BETHNAL GREEN; CAMBRIDGE HEATH
☎ 020 3487 0255 ⊕ THEREDCHURCHBREWERY.COM

The Jerusalem Tavern

This atmospheric pub, a few minutes' walk from St. John's Square, has the authentic look of a pub from a couple of centuries back. Actually, it's been in business for only a couple of decades but has been decorated with the eighteenth-century building in which it is housed in mind, with simple dark wood chairs and a log-filled fireplace—and not a television in sight. For people who live and work in the area, the tavern is a regular spot to stop by after work, but since it opens at 11 A.M., it's also a cozy spot for a midday pint of top-notch beer, such as the remarkable and not overly heavy Golden Ale. The tavern gets especially crowded during the week and isn't open on Saturdays.

55 BRITTON STREET . EC1M 5UQ 🚇 FARRINGDON/BARBICAN ☎ 020 7490 4281
🌐 STPETERSBREWERY.CO.UK/LONDON-PUB

QUICK BITES, BAKERIES, AND GRAB-AND-GO TREATS

In London's thriving food scene, some of the most delectable things to eat are also the least fussy and can be eaten on the go. Many of the cafés and stores that specialize in these types of foods cater mostly to locals, especially in upscale neighborhoods with a discerning clientele, and most have a specific specialty, such as farm-sourced British cheese or bulbous, yeasty bagels. All make it easy to add a culinary treat or two into even the most overscheduled day of work or sightseeing.

Raoul's Deli and Raoul's Restaurant

Little Venice—the lovely, quiet residential neighborhood within Maida Vale that is named for its canal—feels more like a prosperous village than part of a world-class city. In a sense, Raoul's is the area's culinary hub. On one side of the main shopping street, Clifton Road, owner Geraldine Leventis packs the tempting deli with top-quality fruit and vegetables, imported pantry items, breads and pastries, prepared dishes to heat up at home, and not-to-miss soups, including, some might say, the best chicken soup in town. Across the street, there's the cosmopolitan but casual restaurant; the menu pairs European standbys (pillowy omelets, flavorful frittatas, salade niçoise, and house-made ravioli swathed in butter and cream) with dishes inspired by the Middle East, such as a platter with grilled sharp halloumi cheese and creamy tzatziki. There is a second Raoul's location in Notting Hill, housing both a café and a subterranean deli, at 105–107 Talbot Road.

8–10 CLIFTON ROAD AND 13 CLIFTON ROAD . W9 1SZ 🚇 WARWICK AVENUE

☎ 0020 7289 6649 (DELI), 020 7289 7313 (RESTAURANT) ⊕ RAOULSGOURMET.COM

Biscuiteers

At this inviting bakery, the confections are works of art that are almost too pretty to eat. The stars are wafers that are crunchy, buttery, sugary, and thick; they are shaped and decorated meticulously to depict animals, four-leaf clovers, houses and hearts, beloved cartoon characters, and seasonal characters from Santa Claus to the Easter Bunny. Personalized and custom-designed cookies are available, as are decorating classes for kids and adults. You'll also find gluten-free biscuits, dog biscuits, and freshly made chocolates and cakes. In addition to this original location in Notting Hill, there is a second Biscuiteers at 13 Northcote Road, not far from Clapham Common.

194 KENSINGTON PARK ROAD . W11 2ES 🚇 NOTTING HILL GATE 📞 020 7727 8096
🌐 BISCUITEERS.COM

Beigel Bake

This Brick Lane mainstay is a London rarity in that it is open twenty-four hours a day, attracting a steady stream of diverse customers, from locals and tourists in the daytime to club kids stopping by in the wee hours for a hefty, inexpensive fill of carbs at the end of a long night out. The bagels here are closer to those from Montreal than New York City—in other words, they are not oversized and they have a pleasing hint of sweetness. They're also delicious plain, although most customers opt for fillings such as chewy slabs of hot corned beef smeared with pungent mustard, smoked salmon with cream cheese, or smooth peanut butter. Although devotees wax lyrical about the bagels, everything baked here, including sugary options such as apple strudel and carrot cake, is worth a try.

159 BRICK LANE . E1 6SB 🚊 LIVERPOOL STREET; SHOREDITCH HIGH STREET
☎ 020 7729 0616 ⊕ TWITTER.COM/BEIGELBAKE

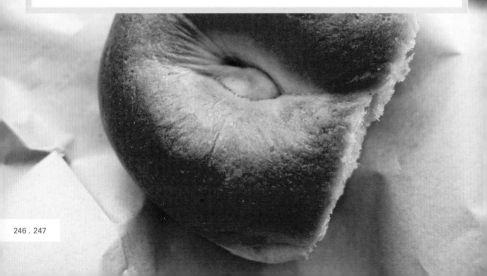

Maison Bertaux

Maison Bertaux, touted as London's oldest and best bakery, has been crafting exceptional French pastries in its Soho neighborhood since 1871. Although the classically baked pastries—glossy glazed strawberry tarts, crusty croissants, and pâte à choux St. Honoré cake—can be purchased to go, the best way to enjoy them is while sitting on one of the handful of chairs lined up outside, with a frothy cappuccino in hand. Another specialty here is wedding cake, available by special order, including a tall *croquembouche*, the caramel-bound traditional treat that is served at French nuptials.

28 GREEK STREET . W1D 5DQ 🚇 LEICESTER SQUARE ☎ 020 7437 6007
🌐 MAISONBERTAUX.COM

Neal's Yard Dairy

British cheese is considered to be among the world's best; and Neal's Yard, which started making cheese in 1979, is many Londoners' favorite source for milky and mild Caerphilly, savory Cheddar, and Stilton striated with deep blue veins. The company sells top-quality, traditionally produced cheese from all over the British Isles, typically from small family-run makers, and the passionate staff is happy to provide a taste of any variety, along with its backstory. Also on offer are thick slabs of English quince paste and jars of pungent chutney that are worth lugging back home. There are shops in Covent Garden and Bermondsey too, but this large location near Borough Market is the most popular for its especially comprehensive selection.

6 PARK STREET . SE1 9AB 🚇 LONDON BRIDGE/BOROUGH ☎ 020 7367 0799
🌐 NEALSYARDDAIRY.CO.UK

Farm Girl Café

Although it's hidden in a nook just off an extremely touristy stretch of Notting Hill, this folksy, health-oriented restaurant feels like a locals-only spot, especially on weekdays, when it's less crowded. Breakfast dishes, which are served all day, are the most popular, including gluten-free earthy buckwheat pancakes garnished with bright berries and sweet, viscous maple syrup, creamy avocado toast, and millet porridge studded with chia seeds. Also available are sandwiches, cakes, and ice cream, both classic and dairy free, and virtuous yet highly tasty smoothies, such as Velvet Cacao, a chocolaty shake that's made with coconut milk, banana, rose petals, and cinnamon.

59A PORTOBELLO ROAD . W11 3DB 🚇 NOTTING HILL GATE ☎ 020 7536 2108
🌐 THEFARMGIRL.CO.UK

Melrose and Morgan

This pair of very cheery gourmet delis—one in Primrose Hill, the other in Hampstead—is brimming with treats that are hard to resist, both virtuous (sour cherry granola) and indulgent (freshly baked cakes, cookies, and rich chocolates). The prices reflect the shops' upscale neighborhood locations, but the quality is superb. Of specific note is the choice of prepared meals for easy dinners at home, including chunky fresh crab cakes with lime-infused mayonnaise and sweet Chantenay carrots mixed with spinach, quinoa, and chickpeas. On weekend mornings, both locations attract families living nearby, who stop in for croissants and muffins and a latte or cup of English Breakfast tea.

42 GLOUCESTER AVENUE . NW1 8JD 🚇 CAMDEN TOWN/PRIMROSE HILL ☎ 020 7722 0011

ORIEL HALL, ORIEL PLACE . NW3 1QN 🚇 HAMPSTEAD ☎ 020 7794 6727

🌐 MELROSEANDMORGAN.COM

Primrose Bakery

This eat-in bakery in Primrose Hill has been specializing in cupcakes since 2004, well before they were ubiquitous in the United Kingdom and the United States. Those sweet treats are still here, in always available varieties such as chocolate and red velvet as well as a rotation of changing flavors including Earl Grey, Toblerone, cinnamon, and salted caramel. There are also larger cakes, nutty house-made granola, and sugar-topped peanut butter cookies, all freshly baked and delicious. In addition to the original location, there are outposts at 282a Kensington High Street and at 42 Tavistock Street in Covent Garden, where cupcake-making lessons are offered regularly.

69 GLOUCESTER AVENUE . NW1 8LD 🚇 CAMDEN TOWN/CHALK FARM ☎ 020 7483 4222

🌐 PRIMROSE-BAKERY.CO.UK

Look Mum No Hands!

This bright and always bustling café is a hybrid—part bike shop, part coffeehouse—and well situated in a neighborhood in which many residents cycle to work. For many regulars, breakfast is the meal of choice, from simple fare such as Greek yogurt topped with honey and fresh fruit to eggs served with onion-laced vegetarian sausages or, for meat lovers, earthy Irish black pudding. Later in the day there are sandwiches and soups that lean toward the healthy side, along with specially selected beers. In addition to the food and beverages, it's a busy working bicycle shop, so many customers pedal here and arrange repairs or pick up a new horn or helmet as well as stop for a bite or cup of tea. As its name implies, this appealing spot doesn't take itself too seriously, even though the edibles and the riding-related items and services are all first rate.

49 OLD STREET . EC1V 9HX 🚇 OLD STREET ☎ 020 7253 1025
🌐 LOOKMUMNOHANDS.COM

Melt Chocolates

Though there are many shops that sell high-quality chocolate in London, Melt is one of the most appealing. Its delectable items are made on-premises, and both Melt stores are permeated with the mouthwatering aroma of molten warm, fresh chocolate. The variety is impressive: tiny feuillantine cookies covered in milk chocolate studded with Maldon sea salt, sheets of popcorn swathed in caramelized sugar and chocolate, and domes of hazelnut praline painted by hand with cacao butter. Both stores hold well-attended chocolate-making classes for kids, teens, and adults and are available for children's birthday parties.

59 LEDBURY ROAD . W11 2AA 🚇 NOTTING HILL GATE ☎ 020 7727 5030
6 CLARENDON ROAD . W11 3AA 🚇 HOLLAND PARK ☎ 020 8354 4504
🌐 MELTCHOCOLATES.COM

FISH AND CHIPS

Although London boasts myriad culinary options, fish and chips might well be the city's most perfect meal. Inexpensive, quick, straightforward, and, most important, absolutely delicious, this British classic appeals to visitors and locals alike. The best of the city's chippies use locally sourced fish of the finest quality; some even get creative with twists on the classic combination of flour-battered filets and chunky fried potatoes. While most chippies have tables to eat in, many devotees insist that the consummate way to enjoy fish and chips is as a takeaway—that is, a "to go" order—although these days the food comes wrapped in clean, hygienic paper instead of in newspaper pages, as was the tradition for many generations.

CHIP SHOP BXTN

Walking through Brixton, it's hard to miss this spirited restaurant, with its exterior walls painted with images of iconic rappers such as Tupac Shakur and Biggie Smalls—and their music blaring inside. The place is great, offering fresh, light fried cod, haddock, and rich skate, plus a full menu of less casual dishes (including deeply flavorful monkfish and chorizo skewers) and an affordable wine list.

378 COLDHARBOUR LANE . SW9 8LF 🚇 BRIXTON ☎ 07894 353561 ⊕ CHIPSHOPBXTN.COM

THE GOLDEN HIND

Many Londoners consider The Golden Hind to be the best chippie in town: a simple sit-down restaurant that prepares classics such as fried cod, hand-cut chips, and mushy peas to perfection, all served in huge portions by a friendly waitstaff. The crust on the fish—almost caramel-colored, with a sharp crunch as you bite in—is superb, as are the homemade desserts. Since it is located near Oxford Street and many office buildings, it gets crowded at lunchtime on weekdays.

73 MARYLEBONE LANE . W1U 2PN 🚇 BOND STREET ☎ 020 7486 3644 ⊕ NO WEBSITE

HOOK CAMDEN TOWN

Hook is a distinctly modern chip shop, with sustainably sourced fish and biodegradable disposable utensils. The menu also veers away from traditional fish and chip preparation with delicious, extra-crunchy results: panko bread crumbs and citrus-infused tempura batter replaces the usual crust; chips are speckled with sea salt that's been blended with finely ground dried seaweed. In addition to this original location, there is another Hook at 49 Brixton Station Road.

63–65 PARKWAY . NW1 7PP 🚇 CAMDEN ☎ 020 3808 6112 ⊕ HOOKRESTAURANTS.COM

NORTH SEA FISH RESTAURANT

North Sea Fish Restaurant is the type of authentic chip shop many visitors come to London hoping to find, offering fresh fish from the city's famous Billingsgate Market swathed in a crispy shell with thick fries that beg for a generous dousing of malt vinegar. Located on a small street in Bloomsbury and beloved by many Londoners, North Sea is quite famously included in "The Knowledge": the list of locations that would-be drivers of London's black cabs need to know to pass their licensing test.

7–8 LEIGH STREET . WC1H 9EW 🚇 RUSSELL SQUARE/HOLBORN ☎ 020 7387 5892
⊕ NORTHSEAFISHRESTAURANT.CO.UK

ROCK & SOLE PLAICE

In business since 1871 and with a convenient Covent Garden location, this classic chip shop is usually crowded, most particularly on nice days, when it provides outdoor seating. Eat-in prices are on the high side here for a filling but not fancy plate of British fish such as cod, lemon sole, or haddock and well-fried chips, but getting your meal to go runs about half that price.

47 ENDELL STREET . WC2H 9AJ 🚇 COVENT GARDEN ☎ 020 7836 3785
🌐 ROCKANDSOLEPLAICE.COM

SEAFRESH FISH RESTAURANT

Located a few blocks from Victoria Station, this shop has served people who live and work in the neighborhood for more than a half century. Coming hungry is essential, as the portions are hefty. The take-out menu includes all the classics, including filets of cod, skate, or haddock, complete with gherkins and mushy peas. For those who eat in, there are less predictable but tasty additions, such as grilled halloumi cheese and salad adorned with smoked salmon.

80–81 WILTON ROAD . SW1V 1DL 🚇 VICTORIA/PIMLICO ☎ 020 7828 0747 🌐 SEAFRESH-DINING.COM

SUTTON AND SONS FISH & CHIPS

As the extension of a raw fish market across the street, this chippie prides itself on serving the freshest fish possible, including varieties such as monkfish and king prawn as well as more typical offerings such as cod and haddock. There's also excellent grilled fish on the menu. Sutton and Sons also has locations in Islington at 356 Essex Road and in the Boxpark complex of shops and restaurants in Shoreditch.

90 STOKE NEWINGTON HIGH STREET . N16 7NY 🚇 STOKE NEWINGTON ☎ 020 7249 6444
🌐 SUTTONANDSONS.CO.UK

TOFF'S OF MUSWELL HILL

Toff's is a true neighborhood chip joint, located in the north London community of Muswell Hill. It's constantly busy thanks to its fresh, made-to-order, large selection of fish, available in traditional batter, simply grilled, or fried in an egg-and-matzo crust. There's the requisite take-out counter, but the appealing old-school dining room is a pleasure.

38 MUSWELL HILL BROADWAY . N10 3RT 🚇 HIGHGATE ☎ 020 8883 8656 🌐 TOFFSFISH.CO.UK

AFTERNOON TEA

The grand tradition of afternoon tea—a lavish spread that customarily includes delicately cut small sandwiches, scones with jam and clotted cream from Devon or Norfolk, and cakes, along with, of course, a soothing pot of freshly brewed hot tea—is an indulgence that's still popular throughout Great Britain. In London, afternoon tea is a meal that's served at most of the city's luxury hotels, but more casual and creative versions of the ritual also abound. It can be a costly splurge, but this decidedly British treat always includes a substantial amount of food and an appealing sense of occasion.

BALTHAZAR RESTAURANT

This branch of New York City's downtown hot spot looks virtually identical to its original Spring Street location, with dark red leather booths that suggest a classic French bistro and a chic clientele to match. Balthazar is open all day—and very crowded before and after performances at the theaters nearby—but the afternoon tea is impressive, with cucumber sandwiches tweaked with a bright green mixture of pureed peas and mint; warm, flaky scones, both plain and studded with juicy raisins; rich chocolate Sacher torte; and pots of Darjeeling and Assam from Postcard Teas (page 120).

4–6 RUSSELL STREET . WC2B 5HZ 🚇 COVENT GARDEN/HOLBORN ☎ 020 3301 1155
🌐 BALTHAZARLONDON.COM

BB AFTERNOON TEA BUS TOUR

In a sense, this is afternoon tea to go: scones, mini-cupcakes, and sandwiches served on tables that have been fitted inside an old-fashioned bright red double-decker bus from 1960 that drives past city icons such as Trafalgar Square, Big Ben, and Buckingham Palace. The treats from come from BB Bakery, which also serves the menu in its stationary location at 6–7 Chandos Place, on the edge of Covent Garden; the establishment also offers a tea service on a boat that travels down the Thames a few times during the summer.

8 NORTHUMBERLAND AVENUE . WC2N 5BY AND VICTORIA COACH STATION, 108 BUCKINGHAM PALACE ROAD . SW1W 9TQ 🚇 CHARING CROSS AND VICTORIA ☎ 020 3026 1188
🌐 BBBAKERY.CO.UK/AFTERNOON-TEA/AFTERNOON-TEA-BUS-TOUR

BEA'S OF BLOOMSBURY

There's no shortage of formal, expensive afternoon teas in London; Bea's offers a lovely service of sandwiches, golden baked scones, and sweet treats in an environment that, with its floral banquettes, is more relaxed and comfortable than a hotel dining room. Priced affordably enough to enjoy frequently, the tea is also a chocolate lover's delight, thanks to the array of rich brownies on the menu. Options for vegetarians and those on gluten-free diets are also available. There are additional Bea's locations near St. Paul's Cathedral at 83 Watling Street and near Farringdon Station at 43 Cowcross Street.

44 THEOBALDS ROAD . WC1X 8NW 🚇 HOLBORN ☎ 020 7242 8330
🌐 BEAS.LONDON/CAFES/BLOOMSBURY

FORTNUM & MASON DIAMOND JUBILEE TEA SALON

This famous food-centric department store serves an impressive afternoon tea in a stately fourth-floor salon with plush upholstered seating and a grand piano, although you'll see more visitors there than locals here. The sandwiches and baked goods—many of which use ingredients that are also for sale downstairs, such as sandwiches with oaky Scottish smoked salmon and scones served with a choice of sweet, fruit-laden jams—are delicious, but the tea itself is the star. There are eighty varieties on offer, from classic Earl Grey to rare Dikom Golden Butterfly, each prepared with loose leaves, precisely steeped, and served in china in the store's trademark *eau de nil*, which is also used on the seating and wall-to-wall carpets.

181 PICCADILLY . W1A 1ER 🚇 GREEN PARK/PICCADILLY CIRCUS ☎ 020 7734 8040
🌐 FORTNUMANDMASON.COM

HAM YARD HOTEL

Tucked within an enclave in the middle of Soho, Ham Yard Hotel is a magnet for stylish types, many of whom come here for breakfast meetings or drinks at the bar. Afternoon tea is served in both the restaurant's spacious, refined dining room, with its brightly printed cushions and colorfully striped chairs, and outdoors at one of the large handful of tables in front of the hotel's entrance. Featured is a daily menu of warm miniscones, pastries, and tea sandwiches, plus heartier options such as truffle-laced macaroni and cheese. Many patrons pair their food with two pleasing beverages: expertly brewed tea and a glass of bubbly Veuve Clicquot or Ruinart Blanc de Blancs.

1 HAM YARD . W1D 7DT 🚇 PICCADILLY CIRCUS ☎ 020 3642 2000
🌐 FIRMDALEHOTELS.COM/HOTELS/LONDON/HAM-YARD-HOTEL

THE RITZ LONDON

The time-honored service of finger sandwiches, scones, and pastries at the Ritz is so popular that seatings begin midmorning and go through early evening for what is billed as afternoon tea. Londoners celebrating special occasions and tourists alike frequent this lavish feast, at which guests are treated like royalty and a pianist plays classical music in the background accompanied by a string quartet or harpist. In keeping with the elegant surroundings, there is a dress code, with sneakers banned and jackets required for men; the price is also high, at well over $100 per person. The experience, however, is sublime, thanks especially to the delicately floral rose Congou tea from Guangdong and the slightly oaky smoked salmon finger sandwiches layered with a thick spread of creamy lemon-scented butter.

150 PICCADILLY . W1J 9BR 🚇 GREEN PARK/PICCADILLY CIRCUS ☎ 020 7300 2345
🌐 THERITZLONDON.COM

THE WOLSELEY

This glamorous, excellent restaurant serves an especially lovely afternoon tea, which is far more relaxed than the power breakfasts and tasteful dinners it's better known for. The tea menu doesn't deviate from the norm—with fresh fruit scones and precisely cut sandwiches—but everything is perfectly prepared, and more substantial fare—such as slightly sharp steak tartare, beautifully presented and topped with a canary yellow egg yolk—is offered simultaneously.

160 PICCADILLY . W1J 9EB 🚇 GREEN PARK ☎ 020 7499 6996 ⊕ THEWOLSELEY.COM

WRINGER + MANGLE

This cavernous London Fields space, which once housed an industrial laundry, includes a long bar, lounge, and spacious restaurant that attracts the area's trendy young residents all day and well into the evening. Every afternoon, a formal tea service is offered as well, with scones and strawberry jam, hand-cut sandwiches stuffed with smoked salmon and roasted vegetables, large slabs of carrot cake and flaky brownies, and Dammann Frères tea served piping hot in vintage china teapots. With its fashion-conscious clientele, it's an ideal place for people watching as well as for a leisurely afternoon repast.

13–18 SIDWORTH STREET . E8 3SD 🚇 LONDON FIELDS ☎ 020 3457 7285 ⊕ WRINGERANDMANGLE.COM

COFFEE AND TEA BARS

A few decades ago, finding a well-brewed cup of coffee in London was a challenge unless you knew about a small handful of specialist spots or were ending a meal in an Italian restaurant that had an imported espresso machine. Today, as in so many cities, there's excellent coffee on just about every block, frequently brewed from single-origin, sustainably grown beans that would impress even the most discerning cappuccino lover. The best of these coffee bars are independently owned and reflect the vibrant neighborhoods they're located in; many, such as Monmouth Coffee, are so popular that there's almost always a line out the door. Still, the British have been known for centuries as fervent tea drinkers, and that passion remains, so bars specializing in Earl Grey and matcha instead of espressos and macchiatos have also started to pop up, offering a similar focus on expert preparation and precise sourcing.

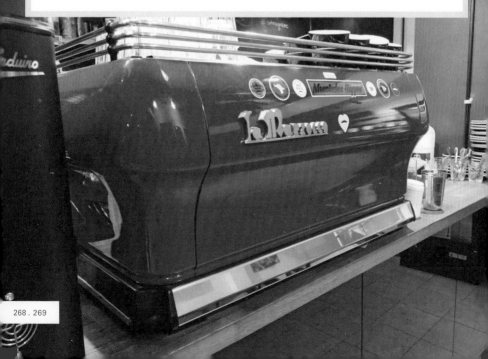

ALGERIAN COFFEE STORES

Since 1887, this sliver of a shop has sold top-quality coffee and tea, along with accessories such as grinders, Bialetti stovetop espresso makers, Grunwerg stainless-steel Turkish coffee pots, and brass coffee grinders. Stepping inside practically takes you back to Victorian times, as much of the decor, such as the weathered wooden counter, has remained unchanged since it opened. Although there are no seats, true aficionados come in for a quick espresso or cappuccino—perfectly prepared and about a third of the price of the same drink at one of the coffee chains nearby.

52 OLD COMPTON STREET . W1D 6PB 🚇 LEICESTER SQUARE/OXFORD CIRCUS/
TOTTENHAM COURT ROAD ☎ 020 7437 2480 ⊕ ALGCOFFEE.CO.UK

ALLPRESS ROASTERY & CAFÉ

This perennially full espresso bar, part of a small Australian chain and the namesake of Allpress's not overly strong espresso blend, is a hot spot on trendy Redchurch Street in Shoreditch, with customers seated and standing outside with paper cups in hand as well as inside its small space. The beans are roasted at the company's other location at 55 Dalston Lane, which is larger and houses a café.

58 REDCHURCH STREET . E2 7DP 🚇 SHOREDITCH HIGH STREET ☎ 020 7749 1780
⊕ UK.ALLPRESSESPRESSO.COM

THE ATTENDANT

Located in a subterranean chamber that was once a public toilet in the 1800s, the Attendant's allure lies partly in the unlikely history of its space. The decor reflects that history—with original tiles and bathroom light fixtures—but regulars keep coming back for the drinks and food as much as for the evocative surroundings. In addition to the coffee drinks you'll find tasty accompaniments, from banana bread and avocado toast, to warming porridge simmered with almond milk. There is a second Attendant in a storefront space in East London at 74 Great Eastern Street.

27A FOLEY STREET . W1W 6DY 🚇 OXFORD CIRCUS/GREAT PORTLAND STREET ☎ 020 7637 3794
⊕ THE-ATTENDANT.COM

BAR ITALIA

For decades, before Starbucks helped turn the world into coffee connoisseurs, this classic Italian espresso bar was one of the few places in London in which to find a perfectly drawn ristretto or cappuccino. Today, even with a plethora of well-known coffee bars nearby, it is still *the* place for many espressoholics, some of whom come for a quick fix at the narrow bar inside. The best tables, however, are outdoors, where there is an unobstructed view of the colorful people parade passing by and heaters make sitting comfortable, even in wintertime.

22 FRITH STREET . W1D 4RF 🚇 LEICESTER SQUARE/OXFORD CIRCUS ☎ 020 7437 4520
⊕ BARITALIASOHO.CO.UK

CLIMPSON & SONS

A mecca for coffee aficionados, this café is excellent and seemingly always full. The attention to perfect preparation, on a La Marzocco espresso machine or a Technivorm Moccamaster, makes it worth braving the crowds. The single-origin coffee is roasted nearby and is served at select London restaurants and cafés as well as in the shop itself.

67 BROADWAY MARKET . E8 4PH 🚇 LONDON FIELDS ☎ 020 7812 9829 ⊕ CLIMPSONANDSONS.COM

EXMOUTH COFFEE COMPANY

Although the coffee drinks here are excellent, Exmouth is more than just a place to grab a silky flat white: it offers plenty of tasty and filling dishes—quiche, cheese-topped flatbreads, Greek salad—and excellent baked goods, such as golden brown cannelles. The constant crowd consists mainly of locals and art lovers coming from the Whitechapel Art Gallery (page 27) next door.

83 WHITECHAPEL HIGH STREET . E1 7QX 🚇 ALDGATE/ALDGATE EAST ☎ 020 7377 1010
⊕ EXMOUTHCOFFEE.CO.UK

GOOD AND PROPER TEA

Tea preparation is taken extremely seriously at this slender East London café: each cup of herbaceous sencha or flowery Bao Zhong oolong is brewed to order in imported Steampunk machines at the optimal temperature to extract the maximum flavor from each blend. Single-origin loose tea to prepare at home is also sold here, as well as ceramic teapots and bamboo matcha whisks. There is also a location at 96A Leather Lane in Farringdon.

THE BOWER, 211 OLD STREET . EC1V 9NR 🚇 OLD STREET ☎ NO TELEPHONE
⊕ GOODANDPROPERTEA.COM

KAFFEINE

Sitting inside this warm café, drinking espresso prepared with a built-by-hand Synesso Cyncra and eating an earthy red pesto and cheddar scone, it's easy to forget that you're not in a hipster hub such as Shoreditch or Dalston. Kaffeine is an easy walk from Oxford Circus, as is its other location on Eastcastle Street. The latter hosts lessons on creating arty patterns on cappuccino foam, as well as espresso making on a connoisseurs' machine made by Victoria Ardunio.

66 GREAT TITCHFIELD STREET . W1W 7QJ 🚇 OXFORD CIRCUS ☎ 020 7580 6755 ⊕ KAFFEINE.CO.UK

MONMOUTH COFFEE
The long line that constantly spirals around the block of this Covent Garden mainstay says it all: Monmouth serves some of London's best coffee, roasted in nearby Bermondsey, where the brand has a location not far from Maltby Street's busy weekend food market (page 181). There is also a third location at Borough Market, with a similarly lengthy queue of patrons outside. Not to miss: the syrupy and slightly sweet Monmouth Espresso blend, a combination of beans from several estates.

27 MONMOUTH STREET . WC2H 9EU 🚇 COVENT GARDEN/HOLBORN ☎ 020 7232 3010
⊕ MONMOUTHCOFFEE.CO.UK

NUDE ESPRESSO
Just off Brick Lane, this café serves sustainably grown coffee that's roasted right across the street. The food is also noteworthy, better and heartier than at most coffeehouses, including airy brioche French toast, eggs Benedict, and raisin and walnut toast.

26 HANBURY STREET . E8 4PH 🚇 LIVERPOOL STREET; SHOREDITCH HIGH STREET ☎ 07712 899 335
⊕ NUDEESPRESSO.COM

TIOSK
Even die-hard carnivores can't resist the flavorful drinks, snacks, and light meals served at this London Fields favorite, such as matcha lattes and vegan date-based energy balls. The tastemakers who have moved nearby over the last few years stop by habitually, while on Saturdays the café is packed with shoppers from the outdoor stalls set up on Broadway Market right outside.

33 BROADWAY MARKET . E8 4PH 🚇 LONDON FIELDS ☎ NO TELEPHONE ⊕ TIOSK.CO.UK

TOMBO JAPANESE CAFÉ & MATCHA BAR
With legitimate Japanese food as its priority, this amiable café near South Kensington's cluster of museums serves a wide range of perfectly prepared matcha drinks, including an irresistibly frothy, just-sweet-enough milkshake. Matcha is also mixed into its desserts, including brownies, cupcakes, and deep green swirls of soft ice cream.

29 THURLOE PLACE . SW7 2HQ 🚇 SOUTH KENSINGTON ☎ 020 7589 0018 ⊕ TOMBOCAFE.COM

LISTINGS INDEX

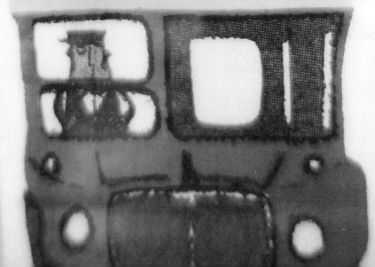

ACKNOWLEDGMENTS

My accent might well be more rooted in Brooklyn than Brixton, but London—Londoners' London, to be most accurate—has long been my emotional home. A solid crew of friends has a lot to do with that. Thanks for their support, advice, and great company while working on this book go to Andy and Shiarra Bell, Kate Holmes and Alan McGee, Amanda Lacey, Henrietta Lovell, Mark O'Shea, Kle Savidge, Jo and Mike Smith, Shelley von Strunckel, and Laurence Verfaillie. I'd like to thank the wonderfully accommodating boutique owners, chefs, and restaurateurs who welcomed me with open arms (and, more often than not, a mug of tea) into their businesses and made taking the book's photos an absolute pleasure. My thanks, too, to the publicists who, in the case of many of the larger companies, helped facilitate access.

I am very lucky to work with an editor as savvy, supportive, and smart as Elizabeth Viscott Sullivan. Her input throughout this project has consistently made it better; and the way she's embraced London—today's London, in all its multi-culti, old-world-meets-high-tech glory—has been truly impressive. I'm also grateful to art director Lynne Yeamans, designer Niloo Tehranchi, and production director Susan Kosko for once again making a stunning book.

Huge thanks go to Marc Beckman and Nancy Chanin at DMA, as well as to Richard Grabel, who has been taking my long-distance calls from London without complaint for a couple decades.

I'm always tremendously grateful for my beloved cheerleaders: Millie Felder (a vocal fan of the Wolseley, Primrose Bakery, and shopping in Shoreditch) and Raoul Felder. Both have been invaluable sounding boards on text and images.

Finally, I hope that my passion for London is contagious; I'm so happy to be able to share my favorite places in a city that means so much to me.

INSIDER LONDON

HarperCollins books may be purchased for educational, business, or sales promotional use. For information please e-mail the Special Markets Department at SPsales@harpercollins.com.

First published in 2017 by
Harper Design
An Imprint of HarperCollins*Publishers*
195 Broadway
New York, NY 10007
Tel: (212) 207-7000
Fax: (855) 746-6023
www.hc.com
harperdesign@harpercollins.com

Distributed throughout the world by
HarperCollins*Publishers*
195 Broadway
New York, NY 10007

ISBN 978-0-06-244446-2

Library of Congress Control Number: 2015945479

Book design by Niloo Tehranchi
Map illustration by Amy Saidens

Printed in China
First Printing, 2017

ABOUT THE AUTHOR

Rachel Felder is a journalist who writes about travel, trends, and style for a wide range of publications. Her work has appeared in the *New York Times*, the *International New York Times*, the *Financial Times*, *Travel and Leisure*, *Departures*, *New York*, *People*, *Rolling Stone*, *Town and Country*, and *Women's Wear Daily*, and on the websites of *Vanity Fair* and *The New Yorker*. The author of *Insider Brooklyn* (Harper Design) and *Manic Pop Thrill* (Ecco) and coauthor (with Reed Krakoff) of *Fighter* (Viking Studio), she has appeared at conferences like TEDx Oxford and SxSW. Based predominantly in New York City, she has spent part of each year in London since childhood and has written extensively about the city.

Twitter: @rachelfelder; Instagram: @rachelfelder